THE SUNDAY TIMES

adding value
to your
property

THE SUNDAY TIMES

adding value to your

Make thousands on **property**

your home investment

hamlyn

Isabel Unsworth

First published in Great Britain in 2004 by
Hamlyn, a division of Octopus Publishing Group Ltd
2–4 Heron Quays, London E14 4JP

ISBN 0 600 60941 3
EAN 9780600609414

A CIP catalogue record for this book is available
from the British Library

Printed and bound in United Arab Emirates

10 9 8 7 6 5 4 3 2 1

Contents

Introduction

This book is about how to add value to your home by buying carefully in the first place, by improving and extending your living space while you are there and by selling well when the time comes to move on. Its purpose is to help you make the best use of your particular property in ways that will not only boost its investment value but also enhance your enjoyment of the home. It contains detailed advice on how to find a suitable property, how to plan renovations both large and small and how to maximize value at the critical point of sale or letting.

This is not a book about the type of quick fixes or house makeovers with which television channels are awash every week. Although adding value to your property and enhanced presentation are not mutually exclusive, they are not the same thing at all. Dressing a property to get a quick sale at the best possible price is largely about superficial cosmetic alterations. Adding value is a much more radical process, involving a thorough assessment of the property and its potential market and, probably, some basic building work.

The British have been a nation of homeowners for only about 50 years. Before then most people rented houses for their entire lives. The original impetus to widespread property ownership came after the two world wars, when people sought security in owning their own property, so that they would no longer be subject to the threats and demands of landlords or condemned to live in slums with poor sanitation and perpetual damp.

Those twin aims – for safety and autonomy – are still with us, but now there is the added awareness of property as an investment. This is not without risk and can be less predictable than many would like to believe.

The old adage 'as safe as houses' suggests that there is no better haven for your savings than bricks and mortar, but in the last two decades the property market has proved to be as volatile as the stock market, whose performance it often mirrors.

For most people, no matter how the market is moving, buying their own home is usually their largest and most significant expense. But property is not a passive investment. To hold its value, a property has to be maintained, redecorated and kept up-to-date in appearance. Most people don't do this adequately, and there are, therefore, opportunities to buy properties cheaply, so that they can be refurbished and resold for a profit.

The rewards of this type of activity can be considerable if you are willing to undertake the work. The cost of moving home can easily amount to £30,000 in stamp duty, professional fees and removal bills on even modestly priced properties. Spending that money instead on renovating or extending your existing home can improve your standard of living now without the difficulty of trying to sell in an unpredictable market. You can tailor a house to suit your own needs and tastes and rearrange the rooms and floor space to suit your own particular lifestyle. Above all, however, the improvements can bring you a profit in terms of the increased capital value of the house, one sure way to reduce the risk of paying too much for a property if you have to buy near the top of a cycle of price rises. It is not surprising that seeking a property to which one can add value is becoming increasingly popular.

But wait: you might not make a profit. Badly executed renovations or layouts that don't appeal to the market to which you are trying to sell may mean you lose rather than make money. There is often no straightforward equation between the money spent on the home and its enhanced value. There are also regional preferences to take into account. Loft conversions may be hugely popular in family-dominated areas of the southeast, such as Wimbledon and Richmond, but in Yorkshire, for example, where housing is in less short supply, they add less value.

It is the hidden extras and the unexpected problems that emerge only when building work begins that usually throw people off course. Proper budgeting and planning can minimize but never entirely eliminate these problems. Overspending the budget is the main reason many would-be property developers fail to make a profit. Falling out with the builder is another common cause of grief, and one that leaves many vowing never to move house again.

Every property renovation is unique. Houses are products of the time in which they were built and the materials then in use plus any later additions, some for better, some for worse. It would be impossible in a single volume to cover all the many decisions you may face during a project, and this book instead concentrates on the principles involved to help you plan your project. There is also advice on what you should be aiming to achieve if you want to make a profit on the work you undertake.

The book also includes pointers on finding a property with potential when you are buying and some of the pitfalls to avoid. It cannot, of course, cover all eventualities, and you should always seek professional advice when you are contemplating buying a house that requires major renovation.

The prices quoted are accurate at the time of writing (summer 2003) but should be taken as a guide only and will be subject to the normal fluctuations of the market and economic cycle. In the last few years the trend has been for the price of building materials to fall, but at the same time the cost of labour has soared, and it is likely that this will continue. House prices can be volatile even over a few months although the long-term trend is for prices to rise.

The housing market is now steadier after the substantial price gains of the late 1990s and there is no longer any route to a quick, easy profit in renovation. But there is always plenty of opportunity for the entrepreneurial or creative minded to add value to a property. Some people even make their living out of it, moving house every 18 months or so. This book explains how you could do it.

Part 1
Identifying Potential

① How to Add Value

Adding value to a property means changing it so that it is worth more than you paid for it. Unfortunately, there are no hard-and-fast rules on how to do this because valuing houses is an inexact science. However, finding a house or a flat with the potential for added value is possible as long as you are prepared to do some basic groundwork.

What is a house worth?

A property is worth only what someone else is prepared to pay for it, and a buyer's perception of the value of a home is determined by several factors, which will affect what your property is worth whether you do nothing at all or undertake major renovations.

Timing

Most people have to fund the cost of their house purchase on borrowed money, and how much debt they can afford to take on influences how much they can afford to offer for a property. This decision depends on the level of their take-home pay after tax combined with the level of interest rates, which sets how many pounds they have to pay each month for every thousand they borrow. When interest rates rise, mortgages become more expensive and prices tend to fall. When rates fall, mortgages are cheaper and prices rise. So house prices fluctuate with the economic cycle.

The first rule of adding value, therefore, is timing. If you buy at the bottom of the cycle and do nothing, letting the property slide into disrepair, it will still rise in value. If you buy at the

Left Many people dream of moving to the country, but you must do your research thoroughly to make sure that there is the potential for adding value to the property. If the house is not located near local schools and shops, or within commuting distance of a large town, your profits may not be worth the time, effort and expense.

top of the cycle, however, you could lose 20 per cent within 12 months, no matter how much you improve the interior.

Property prices rose steeply in the second half of the 1990s as the UK economy benefited from inflation rates that fell to their lowest levels for 40 years and as interest rates followed them down. According to house-price surveys produced by mortgage lenders, this cycle appears to have peaked in 2002, after which property prices continued to rise but at a much slower rate. While interest rates remain low, a crash in property prices is unlikely, despite the warnings of gloomier media pundits.

Over the last 30 years the pattern of property price rises and falls has tracked the stock market but with a lagged effect. The stock market peaked in 2000 before falling steadily over the next three years. For a time property prices carried on rising, but the impact of job losses and reduced wages in the City of London took its toll and property prices at the very top of the market in London started to fall in the autumn of 2002. During 2003 this decline began to ripple out to the rest of the country.

There are marked regional differences in the timing of property cycles, with London and the southeast leading the way and the rest of the country following. At the end of a cycle of rises, the property market in London is sluggish but in the north of England it is booming. There can be a time lag of as much as 18 months before the market in the north falls into line with the southeast. At the time of writing, for example,

Above In towns, location is extremely important, particularly to families with children of school age. The difference in school catchment areas can make thousands of pounds of difference to seemingly identical houses only a couple of streets apart. No matter how much work you put into a property in the 'wrong' area, you will not make up the difference.

although the top prices in London have shown signs of falling, those in the north of England continue to rise.

Many people play the timing cycle in the property market much as they would the stock market, buying on an upswing and selling ahead of a downturn. This may be a good idea for investment property, but it is not a sensible approach for your own home, because the upheaval involved in moving house is probably not worth the potential gain.

If you are thinking about trading up or down to a bigger or smaller house, it may be worth trying to time your move with the cycle. Family circumstances may not allow you that luxury, however, and you should bear in mind that property is a long-term investment whatever the point in the cycle at which you buy.

Location

After timing, location is the most critical factor in setting prices. Areas where there is most demand for property because the local economies are thriving and creating jobs will be the most expensive. In Britain in the last 15 years most new jobs have been created in telecommunications, technology and financial services. These companies are largely located in London, the M4 corridor and parts of East Anglia around Cambridge, and these areas have seen the strongest rise in house prices. London house prices are now about two and half times the value of properties in Northern Ireland, which is one of the cheapest areas in the UK.

Property market experts predict that this trend will continue in the next 20 years and that in the long term property investment in the prosperous southeast will still prove more rewarding than buying much cheaper property in northern England in the hope that it will catch up. There is an oversupply of property in the north, while in the overcrowded southeast there is a chronic shortage of housing, and many low-paid workers are forced into commuting huge distances because they cannot afford London house prices.

Locations where there is rapid economic development offer the chance to add value to property as the population expands. In the next decade the development of the Channel Tunnel fast rail link through Kent and east London is likely to create many new jobs to service the increased traffic of goods and people. Developers are producing huge property schemes to meet the needs of the new businesses and residents that this economic change will stimulate.

Convenience

Within each location the character of the neighbourhood and the convenience of amenities and transport will cause tremendous variations in price, and every city will have some areas that are seen as being better served, better connected, safer and therefore more desirable.

A change in transport links in a city is a dominant factor affecting perceptions of convenience. A new tube or rail line can have a huge impact on property values. Prices tend to move well ahead of the opening of any new links, however, so to profit from this trend you might have to be prepared to live in an area that has poor transport links for several years. Britain's planning system and the complex arguments over private- or public-sector funding of new transport links mean that every new project takes far longer to complete than anticipated. Not only that, but you may run the risk of being directly affected by the inconvenience that a major project can cause.

In the light of these circumstances, you are probably unwise to speculate on improved transport infrastructure in an area if you want to add value to your property. You will have a long wait. If you can rent out a property in these areas, you might consider buying for investment, but transport is as important to tenants as to house owners, and in a soft rental market an area with poor transport links should be regarded as a bad bet.

Outside London airports are likely to prove the most contentious areas in the next decade. Expansions have been put forward at Stansted in Essex, where there are proposals for an additional runway. Longer-term developments could see more runways at Heathrow, Edinburgh and Birmingham. Additional runways will mean more noise and a reduced quality of life for those living beneath the flight path. Any rise in property values from proximity to a better airport could be more than offset by property blight, especially while planning uncertainties remain.

Age and property type

After location, the type of property and its age will have the greatest impact on its value. Bungalows, for example, command a premium of around 20 per cent over a similarly sized semi-detached house because there is a relative shortage of bungalows and few are built now because they are considered an inefficient use of land. Period houses tend to be more expensive than modern properties, but the precise premium will depend on just how old the house is. A 16th-century house might command a premium of 40 per cent, but such properties are rare and supply is limited. A Victorian terrace, on the other hand, may see a premium of 10–20 per cent.

New-build commands a premium of around 15 per cent as people are prepared to pay extra for something that has not been lived in before and needs no work on it. This premium depreciates within the first five years of the property's life simply because there is always more new development. This makes new-build an inadvisable purchase if you are looking to add value to your property.

Condition

The one factor affecting the value of a property where the buyer's own efforts can make the biggest difference is its condition. The cost and effort involved of bringing a neglected house up to modern standards is so high that this will usually be more than reflected in the price at which it can be sold – although this does not always apply if demand for any property in a particular location is strong enough.

Improving the condition of a property can add value quickly. The other factors determining value are slow to take effect and should be ignored if you plan to make a profit in a relatively short period. The only exception is when a property gains in value because the neighbourhood changes quickly. An area may be deemed to be up and coming, and the media creates a buzz that draws people in. This can produce a dramatic uplift in prices in a comparatively short time. Examples of this phenomenon in the 1990s were Clerkenwell and Shoreditch in London and canal buildings in Manchester and Birmingham. These areas were located on the fringes of the city centres, and as old industries moved out they provided run-down factories and offices ripe for residential conversion. They became fashionable, expensive areas within just five years. The same phenomenon can be observed in other cities, including Leeds and Liverpool.

Social trends

In the long term changing social trends alter the value of individual properties. The population of Britain rose by 10 million between 1950 and 2000, and some forecasts suggest it could rise by another 7 million by 2050. Much of this increase will come from immigration, as the birth rate is stable. Demand for an increase in the housing stock will, therefore, continue to rise even though new house building has fallen to its lowest level since the 1920s.

The other demographic factor contributing to demand for an increased number of households is the rise in the number of single households. One-third of all adults in Britain are single, and although not all of these singletons live alone, many do.

These two factors are boosting demand for additional properties, because the number of households is set to increase by 14 per cent in the next two decades, with the number of single-person households rising by an astonishing 35 per cent. This means that much new-build will be of higher density than in the past, which is fuelling an increase in the value of family houses in towns as scarcity carries a premium. Older, traditional family houses offer greater space and larger gardens than can be found in contemporary housing, and they have appreciated at a much faster rate than flats or smaller properties in the last 10 years. This trend is likely to continue, as there is only a very limited amount of land available in cities for building houses rather than flats.

The population is also ageing, and the number of people over the age of 60 is set to triple over the next 30 years. This will produce changes in the value of different types of property. The premium that bungalows already command is likely to increase, for instance, because single-floor living is popular with elderly people whose mobility may be limited. The demand for practicable, efficient flats that are properly serviced and have full lift access is also likely to increase.

Identifying buyers

You should always try to buy a property that will appeal to a wide range of people if you want to increase its capital value. The more potential buyers you can attract, the more competition you will generate. When you are doing up your property, consider who is likely to buy it and direct your efforts towards appealing to that market. Potential purchasers might admire your creative efforts, but they will only buy a property that suits their lifestyle.

The property market can be broken down into several demographic groups, and you should identify the sector your property will sell to and spend your budget to meet the aspirations of this group. Buy the type of magazines they read and visit the shops they use to get an idea of their likely taste.

First-time buyers

First-time buyers are usually either single people or young couples without children. They are generally in their early to mid-20s, although in London the average age of the first-time buyer has risen into the early 30s. They have previously either lived at home with their parents to save a deposit or have shared with other people of their own age. They are not used to luxurious living and have not yet acquired vast amounts of possessions.

People in this group are looking for functional, adequate space in good condition. They will be burdened with a large mortgage because they have only limited capital and will want to spend any spare cash on furniture. They want the mortgage to cover as much as possible and do not usually have the confidence or experience to

Purchaser profiles

Typical buyer	Likely property	Main concerns
First-time buyer	1- or 2-bedroom flat or small house	Borrowing for the first time and probably has relatively low income. Looking for adequate space with functional layout.
Older professionals	2-bedroom flat or house	No children, so larger disposable income. Looking for more fashionable interior and modern fit-out. Spend as much time out as in, so want good local amenities.
Young family	Minimum 3-bedroom house	Looking for value for money. Safety and education of children are a priority. Garden is a top requirement.
Older family	Minimum 4- or 5-bedroom house	Primary needs are adequate space and facilities for a growing family. Minimum of 2 bathrooms. Good schools and transport essential.
The elderly	1- or 2-bedroom house, flat or bungalow	Looking for a home that is easy to maintain and in an area with good amenities/transport connections. Likely to want somewhere that needs no work before moving in.

take on a major renovation project. They do not want particularly luxurious fittings, but they do want something stylish and modern.

First-time buyers will typically buy two-bedroom flats or small houses. In the centre of London they buy small, one-bedroom flats.

Older professionals

This group is composed of second-time buyers who are upgrading. They have more money to spend, and their standards are higher. They expect more in terms of the quality of the fixtures and fittings – they know by now that cheap kitchens fall apart fast. They are also keen to have adequate entertaining space, so the size of the reception rooms is important. They will want a large living room and a decent-sized kitchen.

These buyers will be looking for two-bedroom flats with two bathrooms, or for houses. They will want something fashionable and smartly designed, and good lighting systems, power showers and other expensive extras will add value to properties catering for this market.

You can play around with cutting-edge design if this is your intended market. Single young men who want a flat to impress their girlfriends will want lots of stainless steel, high-tech design items and clean lines. Don't overdo it – not everyone will appreciate your individual taste.

Young families

This is a key segment of the market. Young couples with a baby and with plans for a second child are also likely to be second-time buyers, but they are moving because their requirements have changed. For families with young, growing children a garden is a top priority, and they want three bedrooms at least. Many of their friends will also be couples with young children, so they will entertain at home. The kitchen will be important to them, and they will want one that can also serve as a living room in which family and friends can congregate.

These buyers will probably be looking for houses rather than for flats, and they will be concerned about the neighbourhood. They look for houses in the suburbs with proximity to good local schools and adequate transport into the city or town centre for work.

Older families

House buyers in this group are the key market for what estate agents call 'family houses'. They are couples whose families are complete and who are becoming prosperous. The children are no longer babies; they have their own friends, whom they want to invite round to play. These families are looking for large houses with four or five bedrooms, several bathrooms and a large garden that can be used for entertaining. This group will plan on staying in the property for at least 10 years, so they are looking for quality fittings that will withstand the wear and tear of family life. They need plenty of storage space to keep what is now a vast array of accumulated possessions. Privacy for different members of the family is a priority issue, so zoning the layout of the house is important if this is your potential market group. An en suite bathroom for the parents, a separate entertainment room for teenage children and bedrooms on different floors are all features that are likely to appeal here.

These families will want to live in the suburbs near good schools or, if they live in city centres, they may have a second house in the country or abroad for weekends and holidays.

Downsizing households

This is primarily the retirement market. The children have grown up, so the large family house is no longer needed. The empty-nesters choose to move to a smaller house or even to a flat in the centre of town so that they can enjoy going out in the evening.

Buyers in this group will be looking to purchase flats or small houses that are practicable, efficient and easy to maintain. Their standards will be high in terms of quality of fittings, and they will not want to undertake much work on a property. Security will be important, however, because they are in a position to travel more often and may spend a proportion of their retirement abroad.

The international market

This sector is largely confined to the most expensive areas of central London and to country houses located not far from London. Estate agents sometimes call it the 90-day market because residents tend to stay in their houses for only a month or two at a time.

Properties for this group are the luxury end of the market. Every bedroom should have its own bathroom and walk-in closets. The quality of the fittings must be excellent, and the security should be optimal. Some developers cater exclusively for this market and fill the properties with expensive gadgetry.

You should be aware that this market is volatile. There is the potential to make a lot of money if you time your purchase well, but it is also reliant on the economy being buoyant elsewhere and can be prone to severe downswings if overseas buyers decide to stay home. Different nationalities have different tastes and requirements, and it would be sensible to consult a local estate agent if you are thinking of refurbishing to meet the needs of this market.

How can you add value?

The quickest and easiest way to add value to a property is through refurbishment. The work needed can be divided into two categories: improvements to the structural condition of the house, and extensions or modifications to provide additional or better use of space. It is more work than anyone expects at the outset and can be stressful, and it also usually involves spending money, sometimes in large amounts. However, it can be done by anyone prepared to invest time and effort as well as money.

Work on the structural condition of a property involves improving the basic elements – windows, roofs and wiring – and can also include damp-proofing, plastering and pointing brickwork. Renewing the central-heating system and boiler also comes into this category. Provided the work is well done, you should always see a return on your money for doing any of this work. It has to be done routinely, it is unexciting and people are delighted not to have to organize it themselves.

Improving the function of the house means modernizing the facilities, especially the kitchen and bathroom. It also means making optimum use of light and eliminating fundamental design faults, and includes work done to the exterior of the house and the garden. Beyond that, you can think of adding space through extensions or loft conversions to provide extra bedrooms and bathrooms.

Whether building work adds value to a property will depend on circumstances. In a rising market all properties tend to go up in value, so the effort you make may not be worthwhile. If you want extra space, you could just buy a bigger house. In a slower market, when properties are more difficult to sell, well-executed renovation work will make your house stand out and get a better price while others languish unsold.

The cost of refurbishment

To make money through property you must be organized and have decided on a system to achieve your goals. Most importantly, in evaluating a project you need to have some idea of how much building work costs.

There is a huge shortage of skilled labour, particularly in London and the southeast, and wages have risen dramatically. You can expect to pay around £150 a day per man for any building work. This means that the cost of work may well exceed any increased capital value. Don't trust any estate agents' suggestions of how much the work might cost: they are trying to persuade you to buy at the highest possible price for the vendor. Instead, make an appointment to view the property with a building contractor or relative in the trade before committing to making an offer.

What adds the most value?

There is no simple answer to this question because it varies from property to property. Recent research by the Nationwide Building Society showed that extending a two-bedroom property with a decent-sized bedroom could increase the price by around 11 per cent. Adding full central heating could add 19 per cent in the northwest but only 8 per cent in London.

Second bathrooms are seen as essential in the southeast. Adding a second bathroom in London can add 15 per cent to the price of a house but only 7 per cent in the East Midlands. Remember, too, that a second bathroom is worth much more in a five-bedroom house than in a one-bedroom flat.

The Nationwide did not feel able to quantify the value of a new kitchen, but estate agents are in no doubt that this can add 10 per cent to the value of a house. They regard the kitchen as the most important room, partly because it is expensive to change the fittings.

Example

Three houses in the same street are on the market at the same time with prices ranging between £650,000 and £800,000. From the outside they look identical. It is the state of the interior that makes the difference. So it should be simple to buy the cheapest one, redecorate, smarten it up and pocket the difference.

Sadly, it's not that easy. The cheapest house is being sold by a 92-year-old who is going into a home after 50 years in the house. Damp is running down the walls in the basement, the wiring is in need of total modernization, the heating amounts to 1960s gas fires in front of blocked-up Victorian fireplaces, the lean-to extension at the back should be knocked down and rebuilt, the garden looks like a jungle. The bathroom needs moving from the basement to the top floor to join the bedrooms, which will involve knocking down some walls. The state of the roof and the joists is a mystery. Cost all this work out and you would be better off buying the £800,000 house, even though the agent admits it is overpriced.

Do not spend more than the enhanced value of the house. The most effective use of your money is likely to be a project that will take the property into a higher price bracket or widen the market for the house. Hence the significant uplift of adding an extra bedroom.

How to lose money

The British have become a nation of DIY enthusiasts. Spurred on by a host of TV makeover programmes and inspired by our travels, in the last 10 years we have decorated our houses in all manner of styles from sunny Mediterranean to the exotic Far East: 'a bit of draped muslin, terracotta tiles and we have Tuscany,' cried Edina in *Absolutely Fabulous*.

Estate agents groan. In their view this is the fastest way to detract large sums of money from the value of a property. Buying a property involves an enormous financial outlay, and no one will buy a house unless they think it is absolutely right for their needs. A vase of fresh flowers and some plumped-up cushions will not make a jot of difference to whether someone decides to buy. These are clues to the mistakes people make when they try to add value to their properties.

1. The first erroneous belief is that no matter how much money you put into a property you will get it all back. Many people regard their home as their palace and spend accordingly. But most houses have a ceiling value set by the financial limitations of the prospective buyers for that property in that area. No matter how expensive the kitchen fittings, it is extremely difficult to find a buyer prepared to pay over the odds, and even if the buyer is ready to meet your price, the surveyor for the mortgage company probably won't allow it.

2. The second mistake is to go for the instant cosmetic fix. Much beloved by house doctors and TV makeover programmes, these add nothing to the value of your property, although

---

> ## What goes wrong
>
> You can easily lose out by:
> - Underestimating the importance of size and location and overestimating the importance of change.
> - Making superficial changes.
> - Failing to set and keep to a budget.

---

they do make it easier to sell by improving the superficial appearance. It is a trap to buy a house with a few minor problems and put some money into repairs. When you try to resell at a higher price, you might find that the cost of your improvements exceeds the value of the house.

3. The third pitfall is not sticking to a budget. You have to make a financial plan for property improvements that will leave you with a profit and keep to it. This means taking all costs into account, not just the renovation works but also the buying and selling charges and interest charges while work is under way.

The importance of scale

It is easy to make mistakes when enlarging space in a house by spending too much or by being insufficiently sympathetic to the surroundings or integrity of the building. Although adding bedrooms should, in theory, add value, no one wants a house with seven bedrooms and only two reception rooms. You have to consider scale when weighing up the benefits of this type of work.

Carving up houses that were built in a grander era and staffed by servants has been going on since the end of the Second World War. Many of these houses have been converted into flats, but smaller houses, too, have been divided up to create extra living space in the form of bedrooms. This detracts from the property's value. If a house has large original rooms, they should be kept because the house will feel right. Open-plan, double reception rooms should always be used that way and not treated as two separate rooms.

A small house with two bedrooms and a bathroom but with plenty of living space on the ground floor and basement will always be saleable. There is a large market for such properties because they are popular with childless couples both young and old. Dividing such a property to make four bedrooms leaves you with a family house that suits no one because the living rooms are too small, and the house will be difficult to sell.

The rule seems to be that the more expensive the area, the less impact the number of bedrooms has on the price. Some areas of London, such as Clerkenwell and Knightsbridge, are valued now purely on square footage, and the practice is spreading outwards to wealthier suburbs, such as Wimbledon and Richmond. So if you have sacrificed two small bedrooms to create a huge one-bedroom flat, it should not affect the value.

To gain five bedrooms from a two-bedroom house, half the double reception room would be closed off and a bathroom sacrificed to create the poky fifth bedroom. But with two bedrooms it has a magnificent double drawing room on the ground floor, both bedrooms have adjoining bathrooms and the house has the benefit of a fashionable laundry room.

Further down the property ladder, being able to accommodate people still has the edge over the quality of living space. In cheaper areas of cities, dividing double bedrooms with two windows on the first and second floors creates extra bedrooms and adds between 10 per cent and 20 per cent to the price.

The number of bedrooms is particularly important in areas where buy-to-let investors are active because rental yields depend on the quantity of bedrooms rather than their size. In this market bedrooms are more important than bathrooms, and as a landlord you can get away with a ratio of four bedrooms to one bathroom. This is not advisable at the top end of the rental market, however, where the ratio should be two bedrooms to one bathroom, and if you are thinking of letting to the American corporate market, you should think in terms of one to one.

Example

Two houses in the same street in Clifton, the popular and expensive area of Bristol, came on the market at the same time. From the outside both appeared to be identical Victorian, three-storey properties that had been well cared for. Inside, however, one house had five bedrooms and the other only two. The one with two bedrooms was priced at 20 per cent more than the one with five.

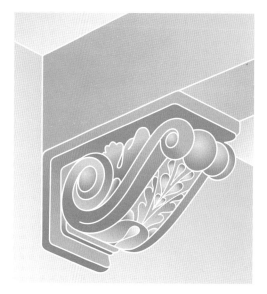

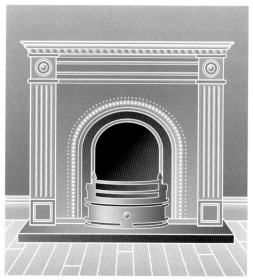

Above In older houses, restoring period features, such as corbels, mouldings and ceiling roses, can be worthwhile. When central heating became fashionable in the 1970s, many people ripped out their old fireplaces. Replacements can be obtained from salvage yards, but a little research is needed to ensure that they are from the right period.

Fashionable taste

The most expensive properties are those that stand out from the crowd. They have something unique that makes them sought after and always in demand. If you can create such an impact, you should see your investment soar in value. But what is this 'wow factor', as the estate agents call it? It is usually one single aspect that clinches it. It is often the view, but it may be the exquisite joinery of a beautifully carved staircase or an inglenook fireplace. It can simply be the period architecture in an area where there is a shortage of houses in a much-loved style.

The Georgian period house is one of the perennial favourites in the housing market, especially in country villages, where houses that were once farmhouses or rectories are hugely sought after. The key is that the house is not so large to be unmanageable but grand enough to have incorporated some of the decorative aspirations of the day. But fashion changes, and here is scope to add value. If you can catch a change in taste and buy a house by an architect who is currently overlooked but will become sought after, you can make large sums of money. A good example is Edwin Lutyens, whose Arts and Crafts houses of the early years of the 20th century have soared in value in the last 25 years after languishing neglected through the 1950s and 1960s.

It is worth looking at the architects of the 1960s and 1970s who are creeping up in popularity but are not yet exorbitantly expensive. Some of the properties may be reasonably priced because they were originally built as council housing or for company employees.

Summary: How to Add Value

Factors influencing value

- **Timing:** most important as the housing market is cyclical.
- **Location:** second most important; areas of rapid economic development are best.
- **Convenience:** character and convenience of amenities and transport links cause price variations within locations.
- **Age and property type:** certain property types command a premium, e.g. bungalows, period homes and new-build.
- **Condition:** this is where a buyer can have the most effect, and quickly.
- **Social trends:** e.g. increase in population, rise of single households, ageing population.

Identifying buyers

- **First-time buyers:** functional adequate space in good condition.
- **Older professionals:** high standard for fittings.
- **Young families:** gardens, at least 3 bedrooms, desirable neighbourhood.
- **Older families:** large houses, several bedrooms and bathrooms, large gardens.
- **Downsizing households:** practicable, efficient, easy to maintain.
- **International market:** confined to central London and reliant on bouyant economy.

How to add value

- Refurbishment is quickest/easiest but may not make a difference in a rising market.
- What adds most value varies according to type of house and region.
- Cost of refurbishment is crucial.
- Make improvements to achieve a higher price bracket or widen the market.

Be warned

- Buyers (and mortgage lenders) will not pay over the odds so you won't necessarily get back what you put in.
- Avoid instant cosmetic fixes.
- Make a realistic plan/budget and stick to it.

② Buying a Property

Once you know you want to move, you should look for a property to which you can add value in addition to having any capital gain that may come through a rising market. This will stretch your limited resources and take you further up the property ladder than you could otherwise afford.

When to buy

The best time to buy is when it suits you, and this is the only rule to follow. Unless you are an expert in investment, it is probably not a good idea to try to play the economic cycle when it comes to your own home. It is just too easy to make mistakes.

If you are lucky, the time it suits you to buy will be in a falling market and you can negotiate an offer. Vendors are, however, notoriously reluctant to take offers substantially below what agents have advised them their property is worth, so only a forced seller will be willing to discuss offers, and that means property developers who need the cash or someone who has already bought another property and has to sell because they are having to service a bridging loan.

It takes a steady nerve to buy in a falling market because you are likely to feel as gloomy and lacking in confidence as everyone else. Don't wait for the market to fall before making a move, though. Falling markets don't happen that often, and many people have sat back waiting for the market to fall, only to watch it rise remorselessly. They see their ideal flat, which they could, at a stretch, have afforded, soar to prices way beyond their means.

Seasonal savings

The property market is seasonal, and activity is usually stronger in the first six months of the year than in the second. The spring is the peak of the market, and the best country houses are put on the market at this time so that you can see the garden when it is looking pretty and fresh. Sellers are less willing to take offers at this time of the year than they are in autumn. Property that hasn't sold over the summer may be reduced in price by the autumn, as sellers are often keen to get the deal completed before Christmas. But remember, property that didn't sell quickly was probably overpriced or there might have been a sale that fell through, so the property might be priced correctly at the lower price rather than being a bargain.

Property developers say that they make all their profit at the time of purchase. In other words, to make money, you have to pick up a property that is under-priced because there is no margin on the cost of building. So, no matter how disheartening it is, keep on searching.

What are you looking for?

The first step is to decide what sort of property you want to buy and where you want to buy it. Most of us buy property we like. Even first-time buyers have a clear idea of whether they prefer period or modern houses, or whether they are happy to sacrifice space for an apartment in a central location and how far they are prepared to commute for the extra bedroom. It is a good idea to stick with what you like, even if the agent offers you a stunning bargain in some other style or location because you may never feel at home in what is not really your own taste.

What do you want?

Before you begin viewing properties, draw up a checklist of the critical decisions you need to make.

- First and foremost, what can you afford?
- Where do you want to live?
- Do you want a house or a flat?
- If you are looking for a flat, do you want a conversion or a purpose-built one?
- Do you want a garden or outside space?
- How many bedrooms do you need?
- How many bathrooms do you need?
- Do you want a period or modern property?
- Do you want parking?
- How important is proximity to public transport?
- Would you accept living on a busy road?
- Do you mind which way the house faces?
- Are you looking for a property with potential to extend it?
- Do you need space to work from home?
- Do you need space to house an au pair or elderly parent?

It will help to draw up a list of what you need from your property. When you start viewing houses, you can tick off where one meets your criteria. This is essential if you view more than three or four properties – it is all too easy to get muddled about which property offered what. Buying any property is always a compromise, and you need a clear idea of what you have to have and where you can be more flexible.

Set a budget

The next step is to work out your budget. This will be determined primarily by what you can afford to borrow plus whatever capital you can put down as a deposit. You must do your homework and make a realistic assessment of any capital you will have from your previous home. There are numerous different mortgage packages available, and you can make considerable savings over the medium term if you pick the right one. If you are unclear about what is the best type of mortgage for you, consult a mortgage adviser who will take your personal circumstances into account when recommending a provider. See Chapter 6, pages 50–7, for more on mortgage finance.

Remember to build into your budget the costs of moving, which many people forget about. These include conveyancing, stamp duty, land registry fees, search fees to the local authority, valuation fees and administration fees to the building society and the cost of the furniture removers. If you are selling a property, you will have to pay estate agents' fees as well.

Stamp duty has been increased aggressively over the last few years, which has made the cost of moving up from even a modest home

an expense not to be undertaken lightly. There are some exemptions on properties valued up to £150,000 in specially designated areas to encourage home ownership in the inner cities. For details, check the Inland Revenue website, www.inlandrevenue.gov.uk.

If you are buying a property that needs work, you also need to set aside a contingency fund for immediate, essential repairs and take into consideration how you will fund the more substantial work you may undertake later when planning consents have been organized and builders appointed. It is important to remember that if you are buying a property that is in need of substantial renovation you will not be able to get a mortgage based on its value when the work has been completed; the mortgage will be based on its current value. If you find yourself in this situation, you need to talk to your bank or mortgage broker who will be able to help you find interim financing or a mortgage lender that specializes in this type of loan.

What should you buy?

In an ideal world, with an unlimited budget, the advice of former prime minister Margaret Thatcher is sound: buy the biggest house you can afford so that your family can expand into it and you never have to move, thus saving yourself all the time, costs and stress of moving, not just once but several times in a lifetime.

Most people, however, cannot afford to do that. They start with a flat, move on to a small house and then buy a bigger one when their family grows sufficiently large and finally downsize to something more modest when they get older.

Current stamp duty rates

Properties under £60,000 Nil
Properties up to £250,000 1 per cent
Properties from £250,000 3 per cent
Properties above £500,000 4 per cent

Houses

A house is usually the best choice for investment. In cities there is a limited supply of new houses because the pressure on space is driving developers and planners to build apartment blocks only, and in the last decade houses have appreciated much more than flats. A house is usually more expensive than a flat on a square footage basis, and you will probably have to trade location to afford one as a first-time buyer.

A house has several advantages over a flat. It will usually be freehold, sparing you service charges and allowing you to determine to some extent when to do maintenance work. Against that, it is entirely your own responsibility, and you cannot appoint an agent to organize building work for you.

Other advantages of living in a house are the greater privacy it affords and the fact that there will be fewer problems with neighbours. If their washing machine leaks, it won't come through your newly redecorated ceiling, for instance,

---

Checklist of costs

- ■ Agreed purchase price
- ■ Stamp duty
- ■ Legal fees
- ■ Land Registry fees
- ■ Search fees
- ■ Mortgage arrangement fees
- ■ Survey fee
- ■ Moving costs
- ■ Contingency fund

---

although you can still run into disputes over boundaries and noise issues.

Avoid buying a house without a garden – it will be difficult to sell. Think hard about whether you should buy a house where there is any problem over access – shared access, for example, or where you have to cross someone

Left With any house, the garden is a vital part of the property. A neat, carefully maintained plot can help sell a home while a scruffy garden is off-putting. Moreover, there is no need to spend lots of money on over-the-top designer features: they might not be to a buyer's taste.

Right If there is an extension on the floor below yours, it may be possible to add boundaries and turn it into a balcony. Expert advice is needed to ascertain what work is needed to make the structure strong enough, as well as permission from the flat's owner, the landlord (if there is one) and the local authority.

else's property. This can lead to troublesome disputes, which you want to avoid. Leasehold houses will sell at a discount and can be good value, but find out if you will be able to buy the freehold or extend the lease before proceeding.

Flats

There are, essentially, two types of flats to buy: conversions from large older houses or those in purpose-built blocks. Purpose-built blocks tend to be more robust than conversions, but service charges are usually higher because the buildings are bigger and any maintenance is more expensive.

Good flats to buy are those which have appealing qualities that cannot be found in a house, and these usually sell at a premium. The height of some blocks means that owners of the upper floors can enjoy views over the city that no one in a house would ever be able to buy. Expensive waterside frontage is also usually

only available for blocks of flats. A flat with a terrace, balcony or some outside space combines the advantages of living on one floor in a flat with the benefits of a house.

Large blocks of flats increasingly offer 24-hour concierge services. This is good security, and the porters will often accept deliveries during the day when you are out at work or let in men to mend washing machines and the like. This is invaluable for people with demanding jobs who cannot get away from the office easily.

Should you move?

According to the Royal Institution of Chartered Surveyors the average move is now once every 14 years. The annual volume of house sales has halved since the 1980s. Turnover in areas that have become family favourites, such as Wimbledon, Dulwich or Wandsworth in London, or parts of Surrey, Oxfordshire and Cambridgeshire, is particularly low as people tend to stay for 20–30 years while their families grow up. Areas like these have good schools for all age groups, pleasant open spaces and reasonable transport into the centre of town for work.

These are the areas where you will see people who need more space as their families grow and who opt not to move but to extend, upwards, downwards and out to the side. The cost of extending to gain a much-needed extra bedroom is considerably cheaper than the cost of moving house. Savings can sometimes be as much as £100,000.

The high rate of stamp duty on houses worth more than £500,000 is also affecting the market at the price threshold. The additional costs of buying a house for around £600,000 will work out to roughly £50,000.

Farther down the market the disadvantages of moving are less and the options for extending your existing property are more limited. In this situation, you would probably do better to move in order to gain the additional space, but try to make sure that your second purchase will be one you can stay in for several years.

Summary: Buying a Property

- The best time to buy is when it suits you.
- Don't wait for the market to fall.
- The market peaks in spring; autumn may be a good time to buy.
- Decide first on property type and location.
- Try to find a property that is under-priced, or one to which you can add value.
- Stick with what you like.
- List your requirements and check them off at each viewing.

Set a budget
- Base it on what you can afford to borrow, plus whatever capital you can put down.
- Factor in all the costs of moving.
- Budget for immediate repairs.
- Mortgages are based on current, not potential, value of property.

Houses vs flats

HOUSES
- Usually best for investment, but more expensive per square-foot.
- Usually freehold.
- Houses without gardens and with access problems can be difficult to sell.

FLATS
- Usually leasehold, with service charges.
- Either purpose-built or a conversion from a large older house.
- Good flats have qualities not found in a house.

Should you move?
- At the top end of market, it may cost less to extend.
- Lower down the disadvantages of moving are less.

③ Finding a Property with Potential

Now that you have decided what you need for this stage in your life, you are in a position to start the time-consuming task of finding a property that is right for you but that also has potential to make money. So how do you set about finding this bargain?

Identifying good value

Bear in mind the rule of *caveat emptor* – if you don't spot a problem with a house, you have no right of redress from the seller. There is a world of difference between a bargain and a property that is cheap for a reason, and most properties that are cheap fall into the latter category. There may be structural problems that are not apparent on first viewing or the location is difficult. For instance, one country house property in Norfolk was offered for sale at a price about 30 per cent less than comparable properties, but weekend viewers from London could never understand why. Half a mile down the road the RAF have a base from which they send out the Tornado aeroplanes for practice between Mondays and Fridays, and the house is in the immediate flight path.

Even if a bargain is not always what it seems, it is still possible to find properties that represent good value for the price and where there is a potential profit. The key is research, research and research. You need to view as many properties as you can bear and still keep going. It can take whole weekends and is frequently dreary, but there is no better way to understand how and why agents price properties as they do and what your options are for your money in any given area.

Ex-local authority

The market in houses that were owned by a local authority but have passed into private ownership under the tenants' right-to-buy scheme has developed apace in the last five years. When the scheme was introduced in the 1980s there was no second-hand market for these properties, but the rise in house prices in the 1990s and a re-evaluation of their advantages – large spacious rooms and solid construction – have led buyers to rethink.

There remains some residual prejudice and a certain degree of snobbery against owning ex-council properties, which means that they still sell at a discount compared with other second-hand properties. This discount is narrowing all the time, however, and in some blocks, prices are beginning to reflect the going rates for a flat of its size and location.

There are still some disadvantages in buying ex-local authority flats or houses. Lenders impose restrictions on the type of flat they will lend on, and generally they will not take the risk of a flat in a tower block and will lend only on buildings of five storeys or less.

If you buy an ex-local authority flat the council is usually still the freeholder, and the maintenance of the common parts and the structural parts of the building may not be as rigorous as you would like. When maintenance work is carried out, the bills are often enormous for the private owners, because the council is rarely price conscious when it puts work out to tender. The people appointing the contractors are not going to foot the bills themselves, so they are looking to comply with bureaucratic rules rather than getting value for money.

Unfashionable properties

Today's fashion is tomorrow's style disaster. The same rule applies to houses as to clothes, but the time span is longer. Today's much sought-after Victorian and Edwardian terraces were deeply unfashionable in the 1960s, and during the 1980s it was hard to give away some 1960s houses. Although there has been a revival of interest in the mid-century, many of these houses are still cheap as their boxy, dated exteriors put off buyers. Updating these interiors could prove to be a profitable investment, but remember to preserve what may come to be defined as the period features.

Today environmental considerations play as important a role in house fashions as does style. Houses blighted by noise from main roads, rail lines or airport proximity are particularly difficult to sell and are available cheaply. Unless there is a major change in local road use, however, you will not see any change in the relative value of these properties. They will always be at a discount to the market, but if you need the space and your budget is limited, they are good value.

Tired or a wreck?

Most people looking to add value to a property choose an older property that is in need of modernization. The amount of work required will determine whether the agent classifies the property as tired or in need of complete modernization. There are, however, drawbacks to buying these properties, which are not always such good value as they might appear.

In some areas the appetite for complete wrecks is so strong that there is no profit to be made on doing the work – the buyer is, in fact, more likely to see a loss. The discount is simply not large enough. Tired properties are more difficult to sell, because they are not sufficiently rundown to be of interest to developers or renovation enthusiasts and are in too poor a condition to appeal to those who don't want to do much work. But to make a profit, you will need to negotiate hard at the point of purchase. Pay close to the asking price and you will be out of pocket.

Flats with potential

Not everyone can afford or wants a loft-style conversion, so don't forget to look at the other types of flat available that offer the potential for adding value.

Basement flats Although basement flats can be dark, this is not always the case, so go and see for yourself in daylight. They can also be prone to damp, and single women tend to avoid them for security reasons, which cuts out a large section of your market. The benefits of basement flats are that you get more space for your money because they gain additional room that flats higher up the building lose to a staircase and common parts. Basement flats usually have a separate entrance, which is always popular, and they often have the added benefit of a patio or garden.

Studios Studios are always cheaper because most people prefer to be able to shut the door on a bedroom. However, one large room can be arranged in such a way that you make better use of the space. It can look more appealing, lighter and roomier than a small flat that has

been crudely divided to provide a poky bedroom where space is so restricted that you fall over the bed trying to get into it.

Walk-ups This American phrase is used to describe flats that are above the third or fourth floor where the building has no lift. This limits the appeal of the flat to the young and fit, and even they will get fed up with carrying all the shopping and rubbish up and down several flights of stairs. If you don't mind, these are good value for money.

Short leases Leases that have less than 60 years to run are usually cheaper because there are problems obtaining mortgages on such properties. Recent changes in legislation have made it easier to extend leases, and mortgage lenders have relaxed their criteria so that the price differential has narrowed. This is a good way to buy into a postcode you otherwise couldn't afford, and you can pay to extend the lease later. Check with the freeholder what the policy is on lease extensions and the likely cost before you proceed. Leasehold extension is a highly complex area; make sure you have a solicitor who has some experience in this area. See also commonhold and leasehold enfranchisement, pages 56–7.

Beginning the search

Start with the local newspaper and the Internet. Local newspapers usually have one day, normally near the end of the week, when they run classified property advertisements from agents and people selling privately. Read these carefully and you will quickly gather an impression of the local market and how much you can expect to pay for the different properties in the area.

If you are unfamiliar with an area, you need to get a feel for the type of property that is available there. Is it predominantly period houses, or are there modern developments and lots of conversions? This will give you a clue to the type of buyers who will predominate – families, young professional couples or downsizing households. You need to decide whether you will fit into this area or whether it is simply a suitable place to buy a property to do up and then move on.

The Internet is invaluable for researching the property market. Nearly all agents have websites where you can search their current database of available properties. Many of the bigger agents have invested heavily in these websites, and you can see photographs of the property, floor plans with room measurements and other essential details. Many agents belong to property search companies, such as primelocation.com or assertahome.com, so even if you are unfamiliar with the area, you can still access the local agents' websites. Before you even approach an agent you should be in a position to compare prices of similar properties and to find out why they differ.

There are a number of websites that are not linked to agents on which buyers can advertise their properties for private sale (see Useful Addresses, page 193). Sellers can sometimes be unrealistic about the value of their homes and use these sites to bypass agents. Sellers seem unwilling to pass the savings on the estate agent's commission automatically on to the

Above Owners of flats in large blocks sometimes face expensive maintenance charges when a programme of major works is carried out. This may depress values for a period. This can be a good time to find a bargain provided you can fund the cost of your share of the building works.

buyers, so prices are not necessarily a bargain, and you will have to negotiate just as hard as with an estate agent if you proceed to an offer.

Estate agents

Estate agents work hard for their clients, and it is worth getting to know local agents and tapping them for knowledge about the market. No one is better placed to describe the likely buyers and sellers for a property and to know the popular features of a building, and what buyers dislike in their area. Although they are appointed to act for the vendor, it is in their interests to get a deal through to completion, so they will try to help you as a buyer if it keeps the deal in play.

When looking at a property in need of some work, do not expect the agent to be fully familiar with what is required – it is up to you to use your own eye and experience to judge that – although agents spend most of their lives looking at property and often have good ideas of what to do to make a property more attractive, so it always worth asking them for their ideas and suggestions.

Estate agents are most helpful when they are given a clear brief on your requirements. If you are looking for a property requiring some work, let them know and specify whether you want to do up something classified as 'in need of complete modernization' (you need to think of gutting the property) or something 'in need of cosmetic updating' (which means that the kitchen and bathroom need ripping out and the whole property needs redecorating, new flooring and, often, new joinery). Cosmetic updating does not cost just a few thousand pounds.

Auctions

Buying at auction could be profitable, but you have to avoid getting carried away by the atmosphere and overbidding. The final price or 'hammer price' in a lively auction can often be twice the guide price, and the auctioneer smiles at his job well done. Despite this caveat, the auction room remains the most tantalizing place to look for properties with scope to add value. You just have to use a discerning eye.

Properties put up for auction come in all shapes and sizes: some are wrecks, some require only modest improvements, some have been badly split up into bedsits and need reinstating as a whole house and some make challenging conversion opportunities. A fair number of properties sold at auction are only partly vacant, and you can saddle yourself with a sitting tenant. These properties are surprisingly popular with young families as a way to get a house that they could not otherwise afford. But it is a gamble on how long a tenant will stay.

Properties sold at auction go under contract as soon as the hammer has fallen, and you have to pay a 10 per cent deposit immediately by banker's draft with completion 28 days later. No second thoughts are allowed. You have to know what you are buying in terms of its condition and legal title, and you need to have your finances sorted. The advantages are that it is a quick and easy way to buy, and there is no chance of being gazumped.

The popularity of auctions has grown rapidly in recent years. Once the preserve of landlords and developers, you now see many first-time buyers and buy-to-let investors at auctions as well. In a strong market this drives up the prices that people are prepared to pay. If you are interested in buying at auction you should go along to one or two as an observer without attempting to bid to get a feel for how the auction is run. Then you can decide whether you have the nerve to buy this way.

Repossessions

This was a popular way to buy a property that you couldn't otherwise afford in the early 1990s, when repossessions were plentiful, following the crash in house prices at the beginning of the decade. Building societies faced with a mass of bad debts sold the houses cheaply to get them off their books.

Repossessions are much scarcer now, although the numbers may rise again if the housing market turns down and people are saddled with debt they can no longer service. (Mortgage lenders do not like foreclosing and will usually do everything they can to help distressed borrowers, so if you face financial difficulties, let your lender know what is happening.) You can find repossessions through estate agents and sometimes in the auction rooms, but they are not as heavily discounted now that the supply has dried up.

Buying off-plan

This route to profiting from property is most commonly used by passive investors. Developers will often sell flats and houses in a block in several phases. The first phase of sales offers the scope for greatest bargains, and it is then that the buyer takes the most risk: you could have up to two years to wait before you get the keys to your front door, and in the

Sitting tenants

If you are looking at a property that has sitting tenants, you should find out what you can about the tenancy before exchanging contracts. Not only will you have to take on the liabilities of the previous landlord, but you might also find it almost impossible to remove a tenant from the property.

meantime, the developer could go bust. The development will be unproven with buyers at this stage, so there is an element of risk. But all this can provide rich rewards if you can afford to put up the money for a deposit because usually the prices have risen by the time the building nears completion.

In the last few years new developments have proved to be particularly popular with overseas investors who want hassle-free homes for their money. This has led to a high number of tenants in many blocks with absentee landlords. With a recent drop in the rental market, many flats have been left unlet or buyers have failed to complete on their purchases. This is likely to prove detrimental to the value of the block in the medium term, because it will begin to look neglected and be less attractive to buyers.

There is, in any case, little value to be added to a flat in a new development unless you intend to gut the interior, which is expensive and probably wasteful. If you are looking to buy to add value, you are probably best advised to avoid new developments.

Conversions

This is complicated and difficult but can be financially rewarding. You buy a large, old house that has probably been tenanted for years and convert it into two or three flats. You keep the best flat for yourself and sell off the others to cover the costs of the purchase and conversion. If you do your sums right, you may make sufficient profit on the conversion so that your own flat costs you practically nothing once the work is done. You should, at least, get a flat that is more valuable than one you could otherwise have afforded.

There are risks in this route. You will need planning permission, and it may take several months to get it, if at all. This will be a complicated building project, which is likely to take a minimum of six months, so you need to budget for at least a year of servicing the mortgage on the entire property and meeting the cost of the building work. If you do not have some capital to start with, the bank is unlikely to help. Budgeting such a complex job is difficult, and you may run into cash-flow problems. The market may change direction between your purchase and sales, meaning projected profits don't materialize.

The other option is to buy a house that was converted into flats 20–30 years ago and is now ripe for conversion back into a family house. As the shortage of family houses has pushed up prices, it can be profitable to reinstate a converted house into just one unit again.

Planning permission may turn out to be the big stumbling block here, however. Many local authorities will not allow several individual housing units to disappear all at once because it reduces the amount of affordable housing. In areas where there is no shortage of houses, it won't be profitable either. But it may be the way to afford the house you really want for yourself.

Self-build

More than 20,000 people opt for self-build every year, although not all of them do much of the construction work themselves. The growing popularity of the movement has been reflected in the increasing availability of resources to meet the demand. There are at least six exhibitions every year for the dedicated self-builder to visit, and a number of general self-build visitor centres.

Self-build demands attention to every phase of the construction process, from site preparation, foundations, pipes and drainage, concrete floors, construction of walls, roofing, plumbing, heating and internal fittings, such as the kitchen and bathrooms, to doors and windows.

Self-build tends to be more popular in the north of England and Scotland than in the southeast, partly because land is available much more easily and cheaply, and these are areas that the big developers do not target as aggressively for new building.

The Internet is invaluable in helping people to find plots. Companies such as Gablecross and Border Oak specialize in buying up large parcels of land and dividing them up so it is possible to buy something with outline planning permission rather than taking the risk that residential use will not be agreed.

There are large savings to be made by doing it yourself, possibly as much as 25–30 per cent, provided you stick to your original budget. You also have the additional satisfaction of completing the work to your own specification and standards. It appeals, in particular, to the ecologically minded who want to build experimental energy-efficient homes with intensive use of recycling and solar heating.

Some of the smaller building societies specialize in providing loans for the self-builder, and the monthly publication *Moneyfacts* lists 36 banks and building societies that are involved with the movement. Lenders have different criteria, and some will lend on the construction only and not on the purchase of the land.

Summary: Finding a Property with Potential

Identifying good value

Cheap properties are not always a bargain. Research well to know why properties are priced as they are. Some are discounted for reasons you may be able to live with, but still represent good value with a potential for profit.

- Ex-council properties.
- Unfashionable properties, e.g. many mid-20th-century houses. But properties blighted by noise from roads, railways and airports are cheap yet unlikely to improve in value.
- 'Tired' properties: negotiate hard on the purchase price but leave wrecks to the developers.
- Flats with potential include basement flats, studios, walk-ups and short leases.

The search

Get a feel for the local market from local newspapers and the Internet before you approach an agent. Investigate private sellers.

- **Estate agents:** tap their knowledge of the market. Give them as clear a brief as possible. Remember they act for the seller, and don't necessarily know what is required where work is needed.
- **Auctions:** still the best place for properties with scope to add value. A quick and easy way to buy with no chance of being gazumped, but it is easy to over-bid, the property may be only partly vacant and you cannot pull out, so you must know what you are buying and have finances in place.
- **Repossessions:** currently scarce and not heavily discounted.
- **Conversions:** complicated and difficult, but can be financially rewarding. You need capital as banks are unlikely to help.
- **Self-build:** demands high attention, but can result in savings of 25–30 per cent.
- Avoid buying off-plan.

④ Location

You can make money in property in any area provided you buy something with the potential to be transformed and you cater to the needs of the property buyers in that area. But estate agents do not cite the mantra 'location, location, location' without good reason. Better locations hold their value in both good markets and bad because there are always buyers who want to live there. Marginal areas are slower to register prices rises when the market is strong and also tend to fall more quickly and steeply in a weak market.

Buying in town

The clearest example of this phenomenon was the London Docklands in the recession of the early 1990s after a speculative bubble burst and prices fell steeply because no one wanted to live there if there was no prospect of a quick capital gain. Even when the property market elsewhere in London began to recover, Docklands was the last place where negative equity was eliminated.

In the north of England property prices have been falling for nearly 10 years in some of the older parts of the industrial cities such as Newcastle-upon-Tyne and Salford, on estates where the incidence of crime is high. Local authorities are now selling the houses off to developers for conversion in the hope of regenerating entire areas.

The best locations in town are well-established residential areas with good shops and schools and attractive properties. If you want to add value and make money from a property, you have to buy something that will always be easy to sell. If you buy an inferior property in a top location, for example, a family home near a good secondary school but without a garden, you can lose money because it will be difficult to find anyone to take the property off your hands.

Schools

Families with children put proximity to schools at the top of their list of priorities, and when you are buying a property with the intention of selling it on to a family, the schools in the area need careful research. Houses near schools with a good reputation will sell at a premium to equivalent houses that are only 3–4 miles away. It may theoretically take only 15 minutes to drive to the school from your home, but it can often take twice as long because of road works or congestion. That journey has to be done twice a day, five times a week, and it does not take long before it feels like a waste of precious time. The dilemma can be even worse in the country than in towns because of the lack of public transport.

If you are buying a family house with the aim of adding value, remember that the absence of a good local school will cap any potential gains. Conversely, if you can find a small house suitable for extension in a desirable area for schools, you will find your potential profits are considerably enhanced by the location.

Buying in the country

If you are moving to the country from the town for the first time, you must be prepared to spend time researching your area. You are more likely

---

Town checklist

If you are buying in a town avoid:
- Flats or houses on busy main roads.
- Anywhere that is more than 10 minutes' walk to a tube station, rail link or bus stop.
- Properties opposite or above pubs and restaurants, which can suffer from late-night noise and even vermin, attracted to the large quantities of rubbish.
- Properties with poor or obstructed views.
- Anywhere it is difficult to park.
- Properties near a football or rugby ground (a nightmare on match days).
- Properties too close to a mainline railway station or alongside a busy line.
- Flats in run-down blocks, because it is difficult to get agreement for refurbishment of common parts.

---

to make mistakes because you are unfamiliar with the area and you won't have such a clear idea of what your priorities are.

The days of being able to pick up a tumbledown country cottage for a bargain price with enough change to cover the cost of renovations are long gone. In fact, the rarity value of unmodernized cottages in England's prettiest villages is such that it may not make economic sense to buy. Demand is such that the agent usually puts the property up for informal auction and is rarely disappointed with the result. Someone will always be willing to fork out for a pretty house and garden in a romantic setting.

Above It is easy to be seduced by a stunning view if buying property in the country, but it is vital to remember that the view is part of the value of the property. Check that there are no short- or long-term plans to put a housing estate there. If a property seems like an absolute bargain, be suspicious.

Couples often move out of town after their children are born, when they want more space, a bigger garden and access to good schools. Family houses are always in short supply in the country, therefore, and if you find one in need of modernization, there is likely to be stiff competition. Be careful not to overspend on the renovation work, however. Big, old houses always throw up more problems than you anticipate, and the costs can run out of control.

Country dwellers are more interested in peaceful surroundings than urban ones, but they still need quick and easy access to local shops and schools, otherwise they risk spending all day in the car.

When you are buying in the country you may have to make some difficult choices. You do not have to reject a property with some of the disadvantages listed opposite if it is otherwise right for you, but it will be more difficult to sell, and the price will usually reflect the downside.

Up-and-coming areas

One of the best ways to make money in the property market is to buy in a location that is currently unfashionable but that is destined to be redefined as up-and-coming. It is always assumed that the trick is to be clever enough to spot the right area before everyone else to get the best bargains, but you don't have to be that smart. Areas change slowly; a couple of new restaurants and a cappuccino bar are not going to make much difference if the streets are still unsafe and deserted at night. You can buy into an area that is already recognized as being on the way up and still make a lot of money as the area slowly improves.

So how do you recognize an area with real potential as opposed to estate agents' hype, even where there is currently nothing but abandoned 1960s warehouse sheds and grass growing through the pavements?

The key driver of change in the use of property in cities in the last 30 years has been technology. The revolution in distribution led to the abandonment of old docks in favour of container ports, and the drift from high-street shopping to out-of-town sites. This has left much greater areas of city centres available to be reclaimed for residential use – hence the phenomenon of the 'up-and-coming area'. The technology revolution is continuing. In financial services the need for huge trading floors in buildings with plenty of space between floors to lay underfloor cabling has led to the success of Canary Wharf in London's East End at the expense of the traditional centre of the banking industry, the City of London. Old offices are increasingly being converted to residential use to provide businessmen with *pieds-à-terre*, and the number of residents in the City has risen accordingly.

So look for areas in city centres where businesses are likely to drift away because technology has changed what they require from their buildings. Also, look to neglected areas close to where business is going. In London areas such as Deptford or Stratford, with quick access to Canary Wharf, are likely to become the focus of residential development in the next 10 years. In Reading and Swindon old 1960s office blocks are being converted into apartments for young buyers who want to live in the centre of town and get away from suburban life.

Country checklist

When you are buying in the country the following types of house make a good investment:

- Those in pretty villages that have a pub, post office, school and local shop.
- Those on the edge of a village.
- Those with easy access to a major road network and mainline station.
- Those with outstanding gardens and good views.

If you are buying in the country avoid:

- Houses that are too far from the station, ruling out easy commuting.
- Houses that are too far from schools, meaning long car journeys every day.
- Houses next to a slurry farm – you will regret it when the wind is in the wrong direction.
- Houses too near a river that might be at risk of flooding, or that are on a flood plain.
- Houses in the centre of a village where parking is difficult and you suffer from traffic noise.
- Houses that are so remote that access could be difficult in winter and, if you have children, they will be too isolated.
- Houses near an airport, because you might find your property designated the next runway in expansion plans or affected by noise.

Right Timing can be very important when buying a property, especially in an up-and-coming area of a town. If just one or two houses in the street have been done up, you will be able to get one of the others much more cheaply than if almost all have had improvements and the vendors have realized the financial potential of their properties.

Key considerations

Once you have identified your up-and-coming area, the two key determinants of value are density of housing and access to transport and other amenities, such as shops and schools. High-rise social housing will remain cheap, no matter how central it is, while period houses in city centres will always be way beyond the average buyer. A third factor, and one that is increasingly important, is the quality of the local environment – hence the popularity of heritage towns, and apartment blocks with landscaped gardens along the waterfront.

Politics cannot be ignored when it comes to considering how land usage is likely to develop. Out-of-town shopping centres, so popular in the 1970s, are out of favour, and now 'affordable housing' is the phrase on every planner's lips. In

some areas planners have recently insisted that 50 per cent of every new development above a certain size has to be made available for key workers or low-income families. This has directly contributed to the overall shortage of new properties, because developers find they cannot make any profit at this level and landowners will not sell on these margins. They can make more money from renting out the land as car parks. Planners may relax their restrictions as they see the supply of new homes drying up.

It takes more than a few new blocks of flats to transform a derelict area. There has to be a combination of new shops, suitable facilities near the housing, such as offices to provide jobs, good transport and recreational facilities. The first areas to come up 25 years ago were pushed through by individual buyers investing in run-down, older properties in inner-city centres where this infrastructure already existed.

You may decide to adopt a simple approach to identifying your up-and-coming area. It is the one next door to the hot spot. If prices are rising strongly in one area, there will inevitably be a spill-over effect into the area that is one stop farther on the tube line or along the bus route. Many people are willing to compromise their desire to live in their favourite area for extra space a short distance up the road.

Always look carefully at the amenities of the area you think might benefit from a ripple effect, as people always tend to champion one neighbouring area over another. You might find that one potential area has good transport connections but is largely overlooked because it offers very few cultural attractions, while its neighbour is not served so well in terms of transport but has the attraction of a thriving bar and restaurant vibe, and so remains the more popular choice.

Summary: Location

Buy something easy to sell and with potential to be transformed to cater for the needs of local buyers. Better locations hold their value in good markets and in bad.

Unmodernized bargains are rare and renovation is expensive. Family houses are always in short supply and access to local shops and schools is very important.

Buying in town

Best locations are in well-established residential areas with good shops, schools and attractive properties. Family houses close to good schools sell at a premium (absence of a good local school will cap potential gains). A small house with potential to expand enhances potential profits.

Buying in the country

Research the area if you are moving from town. Be prepared to accept disadvantages (which should be reflected in the price) and for the property to take time to sell.

Up-and-coming areas

Buy into a currently unfashionable area that is moving up. Study amenities which may cause one area to be favoured over another, such as transport links or restaurants.

Look at:

- City centres where technology has changed what businesses require from their buildings.
- Neglected areas close to new businesses.
- Density of housing.
- Access to transport and other amenities.
- Quality of the local environment.
- Current planning policy.

⑤ How to Buy your Home

When you view a number of properties, often on the same day, you will get muddled and forgetful, and by the time you get home in the evening, all the houses you have seen will have merged into one. You must approach your search in a methodical, organized manner so that you do not waste time visiting for a second time a property that has no potential at all.

First viewing

Agents will usually provide you with their written details, which include room measurements and a description of the fittings, but always take a pen and notebook with you so that you can write down your first impressions.

Second viewing

Even if you fall in love with a property at first sight and are determined to have it, you should not do so without making a second viewing. If possible, take someone with you.

A second viewing gives you the chance to confirm your initial impressions. Often, if you see a house on the same day you visit several others, you might be over-impressed because it seems so much better than the rest. You are more likely to spot potential problems on a second viewing, and it is also the opportunity to decide if you really can live with the shortcomings that you have already identified, given that no property is ideal. This is your chance to take a closer look at the state the building is in and the structural work that will be required, because this will affect any valuation when it comes to getting a mortgage.

What to look for

- Start with the street: What is your overall impression? Are the houses neatly kept and well painted? What types of cars are parked outside the houses? How many building skips (a sure sign that an area is on the up) are there in the road?
- Check if you are likely to be affected by noise from a local school, pub or restaurant.
- Take note of how many windows there are and how light each room is. Once inside, find out if any rooms are internal.
- If a room is internal, particularly a bathroom or kitchen, is it properly ventilated?
- Do any of the rooms need immediate re-decorating? Pay close attention to any woodchip wallpaper, which is often used to cover up defective walls.
- Do any of the rooms need total refurbishment or modernization?
- Is there a good-sized back garden? The size of the gardens can also affect the value of the street.

If you are interested in the property, define the main problems that you will need to sort out to add value to it and work out a rough budget of how much you will need to spend – just think in round numbers here. If you decide to make an offer, you will be able to use this sum to negotiate a possible discount on the asking price. Be realistic when negotiating though –

agents know as well as you do how much building work costs, and if you exaggerate, you will lose credibility and undermine your position.

Making an offer

This is the stage that you either love or hate, depending on how much you enjoy making a deal. You have to start from the assumption that all sellers want to achieve their asking price. They are likely to shift from this position only if the property has been on the market for some time and they have reached the point where they are prepared to negotiate. Even so, they are not going to give away their house unless their bank is pressing them to pay off the overdraft or a bridging loan, or they absolutely have to move for some reason.

Your starting point for negotiation is to establish the vendor's situation. The agent can often be helpful here, indicating whether an offer is likely to be acceptable. If the property is new on the market or if it is in a particularly sought-after street you may find that only the asking price will be acceptable. If the market is strong you may have to bid more to get your offer accepted.

There are, however, a number of situations where the vendor may be prepared to accept an offer. If they have already bought another property and are struggling to afford two mortgages, they may be prepared to consider an offer, particularly if you can promise and deliver a swift exchange of contracts. This means that you have nothing to sell yourself and that your finances to fund the purchase are already agreed in principle, so getting a mortgage will only take four weeks at most.

A viewing checklist

- What is the condition of the external walls of the house? Does the brickwork need repointing? Is there any sign of settlement (indicated by cracks in the brickwork or mortar or a bowing wall)?
- Are the floors level? Does the floor feel spongy to walk on? This will give you a clue to the condition of the joists, although in older properties you should expect some settlement.
- Is the plasterwork smooth or lumpy? Lumpy plasterwork will often need renewing because it has been patched too many times to give a good finish.
- Are there any signs of damp? If you think there could be a damp problem, look at the ventilation outlets. Most damp is caused by condensation rather than rising damp and can be cured if the rooms are properly aired.

- Find out the age of the boiler. Anything older than 10 years will be coming up for renewal, although you frequently find boilers that are much older than this that are still going.
- Look for signs of leaks in the bathroom, often indicated by water stains on the bath or shower surround. You need to be careful here. If this problem appears not to be recent, the floorboards and joists below may have suffered wet rot, and this can be expensive to correct.
- Get into the loft or roof void if you can and look for signs of daylight coming through the roof, which will indicate slipped tiles and inadequate maintenance or even suggest that the roof needs to be completely renewed.
- Flat roofs are notoriously prone to leaking. Check to see if the asphalt is worn and there is lichen growing on it, another sign that it is in need of maintenance.

Probate sales, that is those resulting from terms in someone's will, are another way of securing a bargain. On these occasions a solicitor is likely to be acting for the estate of the deceased, and the resulting funds will be shared among the beneficiaries of the will. They are unlikely to want to wait too long and will be less inclined to mind securing the last £10,000 on the price if it is going to take another six months for completion. Bear in mind, however, that there is always a chance that the terms of the will might be contested and your purchase made unsuccessful as a result.

Other vendors who are likely to be anxious for a quick sale are developers, who need to get their capital out of the property to move on to their next project. They will be keener to negotiate than vendors of second-hand homes, who will invariably have an emotional investment in the property.

Next, consider your own situation. It is not sensible to offer more than you can afford in the hope that you will be able to achieve a further reduction when the survey comes through. At that stage, vendors are notoriously reluctant to negotiate and are likely to offer a face-saving sum at best to ensure that the sale does not fall through. You will have spent time and money on a survey, solicitors and building society arrangement fees, so it will cost you to pull out.

What happens now?

Marshal your arguments for negotiating an offer below the asking price. Apart from being in a position to move quickly, the other points to make are the costs of any remedial works required, comparable prices achieved recently for similar properties (if they are lower) and the overall state of the market.

Start by making as low an offer as you have the cheek to put to the agent. Remember that you can always increase your offer if it is turned down, but you won't be able to reduce it. The agent is obliged to put all genuine offers to the vendor, but if yours is a really low bid, they may tell you immediately that it will not be acceptable. They may, for example, know that the vendor has already turned down another offer. At this stage you need to find out from the agent what might be acceptable and pitch your offer just below what they suggest.

If the vendor turns down your offer, you will usually find that the agent will come back with a suggested price. A tactic that often works is to offer to split the difference. Your aim should be to reach the point at which both you and the vendor feel that a fair price has been achieved.

At any stage in the negotiations you can refuse to proceed and just leave your offer on the table. Start looking again at other properties but don't actually withdraw. You may find that the agent comes back to you a few weeks later if the property is still unsold.

There is a high failure rate of property sales that are agreed but that never make it to exchange of contracts. If possible, make sure that the vendor is happy with you personally as a buyer at the agreed price, because the goodwill will last longer into the conveyancing process. Failed purchases will cost you money, and you do not want to have to pull out unless the property turns out to have flaws that you cannot deal with.

Buying a property in Scotland

The process in Scotland differs from that in the rest of Britain, and is more like that of a sealed bid, where a vendor sets his or her price and invites offers in excess of it. Buyers need to have an agreement in principle on a mortgage before looking for a property, so that they are ready to make a genuine offer the moment they see something they like. Both parties are obliged to complete the sale once a price for the property has been agreed, which eliminates the chances of being gazumped. Purchasers usually carry out a survey before making an offer, and will finalize their mortagage terms once the sale is under way.

Using a surveyor

Before you buy a property you must have a clear idea of the scale of any work you might have to undertake. The best way to discover

Sealed bids

Sealed bids are used by agents to sell a property where there is likely to be strong demand but where it is difficult to establish a value. A reserve price is set, and the agent asks for offers in excess of this sum. You place your offer in a sealed envelope and deliver it to the agent by a stated time. The highest offer gets the property.

If the sealed bid is a formal tender, once the envelopes are opened, the sale is complete. An informal tender means that offers are subject to survey and contract, and the price can be negotiated depending on the outcome.

Buyers do not like sealed bids because they often feel that the process is not fair and transparent. If you are participating in a sealed bid, try to make sure that you or your appointed representative – your solicitor, for example – are present when the sealed bids are opened. This prevents any last-minute horse-trading by other buyers who haven't offered enough. Don't get carried away – there are always other properties to buy if you lose out.

this is with a survey. If you are applying for a mortgage with a bank or building society a chartered surveyor will carry out a valuation, which will assess the basic structural condition of the property and determine whether you are paying in line with market value. Some lenders do not let you see the valuation report, and in any case you cannot rely on it as a thorough or accurate analysis of the state of the building.

It can be a false economy to save on a surveyor's fee. The costs vary according to the size of the property and the number of tests you request. In Britain houses are bought and sold under the rule of *caveat emptor*, which means that if you don't notice a defect in the house, it is your problem and you have no right to claim redress from the seller. An unsatisfactory survey gives you ammunition with the vendor to renegotiate the purchase price if the cost of the work is substantially more than you were aware of at the time you made an offer. You may also choose to pull out of the purchase altogether.

When you commission a homebuyer's report or a full structural survey, the surveyor will be working for you directly rather than for the mortgage lender, which is what happens with a mortgage valuation, and if your surveyor fails to spot a fault, you may be able to sue them. You can also use the survey as the basis of the first checklist you present to your builders and architects of the scale of the project.

Summary: How to Buy your Home

Viewing

- Be methodical and organized.
- Write down your first impressions.
- Always view again, if possible with someone else.
- Work out a rough budget to deal with the main problems.
- See page 46 for a viewing checklist.

Making an offer

- Try to establish the seller's circumstances.
- You may need to offer the asking price or more if the property is highly sought after.
- Don't offer more than you can afford in the hope of a reduction after the survey.
- Start low: you can increase an offer but can't reduce it.
- If turned down, suggest splitting the difference between their bottom line and yours.
- Leave a refused offer on the table: they may come back to you.

Arguments for offers below the asking price

- Speed of sale (especially in the case of probate sales, developers or if the vendors are anxious to move).
- Remedial work required.
- Comparable prices on recently sold similar properties (if lower).
- Overall state of the market.

Buying in Scotland

- The vendor offers a price and invites offers in excess of it.
- Buyers must have finances in place and undertake a survey before making an offer.
- Both parties are obliged to complete the sale once a price has been agreed, which eliminates gazumping.

Using a surveyor

- The best way to gain a clear idea of the scale of work needed.
- Do not rely on the mortgage lenders' valuation.
- Properties are bought and sold *caveat emptor* so it can be false economy to save on surveyor's fees.
- If your surveyor fails to spot a fault you may be able to sue them.

⑥ Financial and Legal Matters

You would think, from the advertisements in the media, that there is nothing simpler in life than obtaining a mortgage. Banks and building societies appear to want to give money away. The reality is likely to be a little different. You are applying to borrow a large sum of money, and lenders will be anxious to protect their interests.

Raising the money

When you try to borrow money from a bank or building society you will be subject to a battery of credit checks and enquiries about your exact financial status and recent employment history. You will have to fill in endless forms, and all the information must be accurate or you will be potentially liable for fraud.

There is a daunting array of choice in the mortgage market, and you should take a little time to do your homework. Your mortgage is likely to be your biggest monthly expense for many years, and even small variations in rates can make a large difference to your monthly outgoings.

A mortgage involves payment of interest on the loan and repayment of the capital borrowed. The two elements are often split. You should try to find the cheapest interest rate available, but remember that this will usually come with strings attached, such as redemption penalties if you redeem the loan early or compulsory insurance, which is generally more expensive than is available elsewhere. Try to avoid incurring these penalties, because you do not know how your circumstances may change.

Types of mortgage

Make sure that the type of mortgage you take out is suitable for both your present circumstances and any foreseeable changes in the short term.

Repayment mortgages A repayment mortgage involves monthly payments covering both interest and capital. The term of the loan is usually 25 years. This type of mortgage is simple to understand, and there is no risk attached other than your ability to keep up with the monthly payments.

Interest-only mortgages When you take out this type of mortgage you make monthly payments that cover the interest only. You are responsible for finding the capital at the end of the term. These are cheaper than repayment mortgages and are useful for first-time buyers, who rarely pay off much capital before moving to a bigger property.

Endowment mortgages An endowment mortgage requires you to make monthly payments of the interest, while repayment of the capital borrowed is funded by monthly premiums into an endowment policy, which will mature at the end of the term. An element of life cover is included in the premiums, so the sum assured is paid out on death. The endowment depends on the performance of the stock market to build up a large enough sum. Returns have been disappointing in the last few years, and some policies have been unable to repay the mortgage in full, so they are less popular than they were.

ISA mortgages ISA (individual savings account) mortgages are the same as endowment policies except that premiums are invested in an ISA savings vehicle, where no capital gains will be paid on profits. ISAs are cheaper than endowments because charges are lower and there is no life cover premium. Their value fluctuates with the stock market.

Pension mortgages These mortgages are similar to endowments, but the pension premiums attract tax relief. Investments in the pension fund are dependent on the performance of the stock market.

Flexible mortgages This type of mortgage is usually run in conjunction with a savings account or even a current account. You can make underpayments or overpayments as and when it suits you without incurring penalties. You can offset interest from your savings account against the interest charged on your mortgage, which is tax efficient, especially for higher-rate taxpayers. This is a particularly attractive product for self-employed people, whose income tends to fluctuate, or for people who receive large annual bonuses and want to reduce the mortgage by paying in lump sums from time to time.

Discount mortgages This type of mortage is offered at a below-market rate of interest for a limited period, usually from six months to three years, after which the rate reverts to the standard rate. You will usually incur redemption penalties for a period after the discount ends if you pay off the mortgage and move elsewhere.

Tracker mortgages A tracker mortgage involves making monthly repayments that track the Bank of England's base rate and so rise and fall with interest rates. The rate is cheaper than the standard variable rate (see below) but it is not as attractive as a discount mortgage rate (see page 51). The advantage is that trackers can run for the life of the mortgage, so there are usually no tie-ins.

Interest rates

Not only are there several types of mortgage, it is possible to find different interest rates, which directly affect your monthly repayments.

Variable rate This is the standard rate, which each lender sets. It is related to the Bank of England's base rate – it usually about 1.5 per cent higher – but does not necessarily rise or fall every time the Bank changes rates. The borrower shoulders all the risk of any movement in interest rates, which can be painful if interest rates rise steeply in a short period.

Fixed rate A fixed-rate mortgage is one where the interest for monthly repayments is set for a period, usually between two and five years. This provides stability in the early years of the term. The disadvantage is that payments don't fall if interest rates fall. The government is keen to see fixed-rate mortgages extended for the full term of the mortgage, but this is likely to prove more expensive than a system based on variable rates.

Capped rate Capped rates are similar to fixed rates, but they have the advantage that the monthly rate falls if interest rates fall. They are popular when interest rates are on an upward trend because the rate does not rise with interest rates. This can give you the best of both worlds, but the cap is usually for a limited period only.

How much can you borrow?

The size of mortgage that a lender will grant on a property is determined by your income, by the value of the property and by your individual

Islamic mortgages

The majority of mortgages available in Britain do not comply with Islamic law, which makes it difficult for Muslims to borrow. In the simplest terms, Islam does not accept the principles of paying interest, because it allows one party to gain financially at another's expense. This conflicts with the belief that wealth creation should be based on a partnership in which risks and rewards are shared fairly between the two parties.

In order to overcome the problem, it is possible to arrange an Islamic mortgage (currently available from the United Bank of Kuwait and the West Bromwich Building Society, and likely to become more widespread). Under the terms of the mortgage the lender buys a property on the purchaser's behalf, who then pays rent to the lender until the final instalment, by which time the purchaser owns the property in their own right.

credit history. You can borrow a multiple of your salary – usually three or four times – and bonuses are also taken into account, although with less generous multiples. If you are a couple, the usual formula is either two-and-a-half times the joint income or three times the major income and one times the lower income.

Some lenders offer multiples of as much as six times income, although the criteria are strict, and these are likely to be available only to people with excellent credit records and good job prospects, who can be expected to bring the multiple down in a relatively short period.

Some banks and building societies now use an affordability measure rather than just income multipliers. The figure is assessed on your incomings and outgoings, and usually results in a bigger loan than is available from your income. It is useful for first-time buyers, who tend to have fewer commitments than families, but be careful not to over-commit yourself.

Another factor affecting the mortgage you can raise is the value of the property. Lenders prefer to lend 75–90 per cent of the property's value, as assessed by their valuer. If you want a higher loan-value ratio, you will have to pay a higher interest rate. On the other hand, you won't get a lower interest rate if you can offer more than 25 per cent equity in the property, but lenders may be more relaxed about income multiples.

You can obtain a mortgage from any bank or building society by simply making an appointment to see a mortgage adviser, and the only charges are likely to be a small arrangement fee and the cost of the valuation report. You will, however, be able to choose only from their selected range of mortgages. If you want to choose from across the market you should approach a mortgage broker. They track all the mortgage offers from all the banks and often have special exclusive deals from lenders at attractive rates. You will usually have to pay a fee for their service, which will be about 1 per cent of the value of the property.

If you don't want to pay a mortgage broker's fee you can research the market yourself. A good place to start is with the 'best buy' tables printed in the personal finance sections of many newspapers. They give a good idea of the current best offers in different sections of the mortgage market. There are also a number of specialist magazines that provide a more comprehensive list of mortgage offers. The Internet is an invaluable resource, although it can be time-consuming.

First-time buyers

The most difficult property purchase to fund is always the first one. The rise in house prices over the last five years has made it even tougher for young people to raise a large enough deposit to make that initial step while they are paying rent. There are a number of things they can do to overcome the hurdles.

Parental assistance

Many parents are keen to help their children get started on the property ladder by making a contribution to the deposit or lending some money. They can remortgage their own home to raise the cash, and if they shop around carefully, the additional payments on the mortgage need not be much more than they are already paying.

Poor credit history

If you are self-employed and cannot point to a regular income stream to meet monthly repayments or if you have ever had a county court judgement against you for debt you may find it hard to obtain a standard mortgage. You need to go to one of the specialist providers who cater for such a market. You will find details in the specialist mortgage magazines. You may have to pay a higher rate of interest.

Another option is for parents to act as guarantors of the loan so that the children can get a bigger loan. This does leave the parents liable for the debt if the borrowers – their children – default, so this is a solution only when children have a good, secure relationship with their parents.

New-builds

Developers have to get their flats sold to generate cash, and if the market is sticky or they are trying to sell off the last few remaining flats in a block, they will offer incentives to buyers, which may include paying a first-time buyer's deposit, usually 5 per cent. Other developers may pay the mortgage for the first year. Negotiate hard and you might find that stamp duty and legal fees will also be met. Do check to make sure that the developer is not going to make up for their generosity through hefty service charges or other fees.

First-time buyer mortgages

Many banks and building societies offer cheaper mortgages to first-time buyers to draw them in. Some financial providers offer 100 per cent mortgages or sometimes up to 125 per cent to help with the cost of furnishing the property. These are not the cheapest mortgages available, however, and you should make sure that there are no redemption penalties. If the property rises in value in the first year or two of ownership, you will be able to remortgage at a cheaper rate because you will have some equity. With a deposit of only 5 per cent, you can get significantly cheaper mortgages than with a full loan.

Do not pay the mortgage indemnity guarantee, which protects the lender against the risk of the borrower defaulting on the loan. These are expensive premiums and unpopular. Most lenders no longer insist on the payment.

Co-ownership

As house prices have soared young people are increasingly clubbing together to buy properties. They have the fun of living together rather than living alone in a small, poky flat, so this can appear to be an attractive option. There are potential problems, however. The first and most likely is that you might fall out with your friends when you live under the same roof.

All borrowers on the mortgage are jointly and severally liable for the combined mortgage payments, so if one of the house owners loses their job and heads off to Australia for a year, the others are responsible for that portion of the mortgage as well as for their own.

Another difficulty arises when it comes to

selling the property. If one co-owner wants to leave, the others have to buy them out, which they may not be able to afford to do even if they can reach agreement on the value. The only alternative is to sell the whole property, which may not suit those who want to stay. It is imperative that you draw up an agreement between all of you at the outset about how to proceed in such circumstances.

Buying a property

Once your offer for a property has been accepted, you should appoint a solicitor to handle the conveyancing. Although you can do it yourself, it is not advisable especially if the property is leasehold. If you do not have a solicitor, ask the estate agent to refer you to someone they know.

Always ask the cost at the outset. A solicitor's charges are usually based on a minimum fee, which may vary depending on the price and type of property you are buying. In addition there will be disbursements, which you will have to meet. These include Land Registry fees, search fees and VAT.

The legal commitment to purchase a property is made at the time of exchange of contracts not on the completion day, which is when you move. Before exchange you are entitled to pull out at any time without penalty. This allows you time to arrange the mortgage finance, survey and search the property for potential problems. In Scotland, the house buying process is different and use of sealed bids is common practice. If your offer is accepted, it is binding on both parties. You carry out the survey and searches before putting in an offer.

The seller's solicitor issues a draft contract of sale and provides documents such as title deeds, copies of the lease and a seller's property information form. This requires the seller to declare the fixtures and fittings that will be included in the sale, and a history of maintenance on the house.

Seller's packs

The seller's property information form is not yet a legal requirement but if the proposal to introduce seller's packs becomes law, disclosure of this information will be mandatory. The seller's pack will require the seller to prepare a survey and organize searches before marketing the property. This is designed to speed up the process of house purchase. The searches from the local authority will show whether any changes to the property comply with planning requirements and whether there is any scheduled development in the area, which might affect its value.

The solicitor's aim is to establish that the title is sound, and that the boundaries are well defined with no scope for dispute. He will point out to you any defects he sees in the title or the lease and advise on whether you should proceed with the sale or not. If he fails to spot a major legal defect, he will be liable for negligence.

Once both sides are happy and satisfied with the answers to enquiries, you are ready to proceed to exchange of contract. At this point, you have to pay a deposit of 10 per cent of the purchase price unless a smaller sum is agreed. You then have up to 28 days to complete the purchase although it is common now to complete after 14 days.

The solicitor will arrange completion for you. This involves organizing the release of funds from the mortgage company, organising insurance for the building and that the terms of the contract are all fulfilled. Once the seller's solicitor has the money in his account, the keys are released.

Commonhold

The Commonhold and Leasehold Reform Act 2002, which was in the process of being implemented at the time of writing, is likely to have implications for the capital value of flats in developments when fully operational.

Commonhold introduces a different structure of ownership from the traditional freehold and leasehold and will allow flats in a development to be owned on a permanent and time-limited basis. The principal benefit is that the owners of the flats have a permanent interest in their property, and the value of the lease will not diminish over time as a lease does, especially towards the end of its life. This will help to improve the market value of the property.

Commonhold is also designed to end the disadvantages of the landlord-tenant relationship, which has bedevilled the management of many large blocks of flats, with complaints of high service charges and inadequate maintenance. Each flat owner will be deemed to be a unit-holder and a member, with the other unit-holders, of the commonhold association, which will own and manage the common parts and facilities of the development. This arrangement should lead to blocks being better cared for, with consequent implications for enhanced capital value.

Leasehold enfranchisement

The same act has also made it much easier to obtain leasehold enfranchisement. This is where flat owners in a block club together to buy the freehold of the property or where an individual flat owner obtains an extension to his lease. The law used to stipulate that tenants must meet residency qualifications in the flat before they were entitled to an automatic lease extension, but the rules have been greatly relaxed under the new Act, making it simpler and quicker to apply.

Anyone who holds a long lease on a flat – that is, an original term of 21 years or more – can require the landlord to grant a new lease, extending the term for a fixed period of 90 years, provided that he has held the lease for at least two years. There is no longer any residency test, so corporate lessees and investors who have never lived in the property can now take advantage of the right to extend.

The rules for leasehold houses are similar to flats, and a tenant may want to acquire the freehold. There are some exclusions, so consult a solicitor to check that you will be able to proceed.

The cost of a new lease is normally determined by negotiation between the landlord and tenant, but if the parties cannot reach agreement, the Leasehold Valuation Tribunal settles the dispute, and the tenant will have to meet the landlord's legal and valuation costs. The marriage value (the difference between the value of the existing lease and the new extended lease or freehold) is now split equally between the two parties rather than the landlord charging the entire difference, as was the case in the past. If the existing lease has more than 80 years to run, the marriage value is deemed to be nil.

Summary: Financial and Legal Matters

Raising the money

To borrow money you will be subject to credit checks and enquiries about your recent financial and employment status. Research well and try to find a mortgage that suits your present circumstances as well as forseeable changes.

A mortgage involves payment of interest on the loan and repayment of capital borrowed. The two elements may be split, as they are in Interest Only, Endowment, ISA and Pension mortgages. Mortgages involving repayment of both elements are Repayment and Flexible. Tracker mortgages can be either repayment or interest only. The rate of interest you pay on all mortgages may be Variable, Fixed or Capped.

How much you can borrow is determined by your income, the value of the property and your credit history. Find out about mortgages from a bank or building society (they will sell only their products), pay a mortgage broker or do your own research in newspapers, specialist magazines and the Internet.

First-time buyers

The first property purchase is always the hardest to fund. If you can, get parental assistance in the form of capital for a deposit or standing guarantors of the loan. Special first-time buyer mortgages are sometimes cheaper and some offer 100 per cent (or more), but they may carry redemption penalties and may not be cheap in the long run. Developers offer incentives on new-builds.

Buying with others – co-ownership – is another solution. All borrowers are jointly and severally liable for combined payments, so always draw up an agreement at the outset about how to proceed in the event of disagreement.

⑦ Planning the Renovation

Defining your objectives | Preparing a brief | Setting a budget
Managing the project | Employing a project manager
Using an architect | Appointing a builder | Scheduling the work
Avoiding common problems | Getting planning permission
Restoring a listed building | Obtaining grants

⑧ Creating Space

The rules of layout | Adding value through redesign
Planning considerations | Loft conversions | Basement conversions
Back extensions | Garage conversions | Porch conversions
Building a conservatory | Converting entire buildings

⑨ Making Improvements

Subsidence | Drains | Damp-proofing | Walls and brickwork
Windows | Joists | Roofs | Central heating | Wiring | Staircases

Part 2
Refurbishing your Home

⑦ Planning the Renovation

The relationship between builders and clients is, notoriously, a bad one. Customers complain about bad workmanship and poor time-keeping. Builders complain about indecisive customers who change their minds every day, have unrealistic expectations of how long the work should take and pay late. Having the builders in can be as stressful as moving house and just as likely to precipitate divorce.

Defining your objectives

Before you even think about appointing builders, you need to decide on your objectives for the property because they will determine how much time and money you want to invest in it. The list opposite summarizes the key issues.

If you intend to live in the property for only a few years, you need to consider carefully how much value your renovations will add and make sure that the work will be profitable. If you plan to stay for the next 20 years, you can clearly spend with a free hand because you are doing the work for your own enjoyment as well as for investment. Moreover, if you are planning to stay for many years, you can plan alterations to be carried out over a number of years. You should, however, make sure that work you do now will not have to be undone if you decide later that you need to do other work.

If the use of your home is likely to change as you start a family or switch to working from home, the layout of the rooms should be flexible so that alterations can be carried out with minimum cost as your needs change.

If you are planning to renovate the house for profit or to rent it out, you need the work to be to a standard that does not compromise its value. This calls for careful judgement in setting your budget: the cheapest will not necessarily be the best choice. For rental properties, however, you don't want to overspend because the tenants will not look after it as well as you would if you were living there yourself.

Bearing in mind the answers to the questions about the property's long-term use, ask yourself the questions listed on the right as you begin to consider how well the house functions as it is currently laid out and how well the space is used. If the answer to any of these questions is 'no', then you need to consider some redesign of the house and, possibly, the addition of new space.

Preparing a brief

It is an inconvenient fact, but you must remember that the work you want to undertake first – that is, the work that will make the biggest difference to your comfort, such as a new kitchen – may have to come last. This is because essential structural works have to be done first so that the basics are in place before you start spending on expensive fittings. Hence the importance of planning and scheduling to make sure that everything is done in the right order so that you do not waste money by having to redo work.

Before you approach an architect or surveyor, or, if you are organizing the project yourself, a builder, you need to prepare a brief. This should be a comprehensive list of all the works you need to undertake – wiring,

Key questions on long-term use

- How do you think of your house? Is it a private retreat for the end of a busy day, is it a place for entertaining on a grand scale or is it going to be the centre for a busy and lively family?
- How long do you intend to live in the property? Do you plan to sell after a short time? Is this a home for three to five years before you plan to buy somewhere bigger or is this your family home for the next 20 years?
- How do you use your home and how might this change in coming years? Do you currently live and work at home or do you intend to do so in the future?
- Do you intend to expand the size of your family while you are living in this house?
- Do you have to consider older family members who might need to stay for lengthy periods?
- If you are renovating for profit, who do you think are the likely buyers for this type of property and what qualities will they be looking for?
- Do you plan to rent out the property?
- How would you like the property to appear?

Key questions on layout

- Are you making the most efficient use of the available space?
- Are any rooms unused?
- Are the areas that are designated for socializing and those for privacy effectively zoned in the layout?
- Are the working rooms – the bathroom and kitchen, for example – in the best positions for serving the rest of the house?
- Are the bathrooms near to the bedrooms?
- Can everyone get out of the house quickly in the morning without falling over each other in the bathroom and kitchen?

plumbing, damp-proofing and so on – and the things you would like to do that may involve erecting or demolishing walls or simply redecoration and improving storage. Even if you cannot afford to do all the work in one go, you should put everything down on paper so that you can structure the order in which the work should proceed.

What needs doing?

Start with the structural considerations. What defects need to be corrected and where are urgent repairs required? If there is dry rot or damp, for instance, this should be tackled as a matter of urgency because leaving it will make the problems worse. Check the roof at this stage, too. What state is it in? What is the likely extent of repair?

Is the wiring and the plumbing old and in need of modernization? Wiring should not really be more than 25 years old because it becomes increasingly dangerous as the wires become brittle with age. Boilers become inefficient and expensive when they are over 10 years old. A new one will cut down your heating bills considerably and probably save energy, because the technology is improving all the time. Work on central heating and wiring will be messy and complicated. It will probably involve lifting floorboards and removing large amounts of plaster, so this is best done in the early stages of a renovation.

You need to consider whether your house complies with current building regulations, which are getting stricter all the time. Although you need not reinstate walls that were knocked out 30 years ago but could not be taken down now because of new fire rules, you do need to take into account the up-to-date regulations on windows and boiler flues. Your house may not pass a structural survey if you do not comply with current regulations.

Do not forget aesthetic considerations, which will give you pleasure from the property. What do you want the house to look like? Do you, for example, want to spend money replacing original features in a Victorian property?

The checklist opposite will help you organize your brief.

Setting a budget

The first consideration – and frequently a stumbling block – is money. When you are planning a project you need an accurate,

A briefing checklist

When you are preparing a brief, use the following to help you organize your initial ideas of what needs to be done and what you would like to be done:

External
- Walls, including rebuilding bowing walls, repointing, repairing cracks and defective render, repairing defective lintels.
- Roof, including replacing slates and flashing, replacing old guttering, rebuilding or removing old, unsafe chimneystacks, capping the chimney.
- Carrying out maintenance and re-asphalting flat roofs; improving coving on parapet walls.
- Renewing rotten windows or replacing in a style appropriate to the age of the house.

Cosmetic
- Renewing the kitchen and bathrooms.
- Replastering.
- Redecorating.
- Renewing internal joinery, including doors.
- Improving storage.
- Rearranging rooms to improve the property's functional efficiency.

Structural
- Damp-proofing.
- Repairing or renewing drainage systems.
- Replacing old wiring or adding new circuits.
- Installing a new boiler and installing or upgrading the central-heating system.
- Removing the cold-water tank and running the water system directly from the mains supply.
- Renewing joists, floorboards, staircases and skirting boards.

Changing layouts
- Making repairs and correcting defects.
- Enhancing existing space through redecoration, use of colour and furnishings.
- Rearranging existing space by adding or removing walls and doors and adding or removing windows.
- Converting unused space, such as the attic, garage or basement, into living space.
- Adding extra space, such as a new room or another floor, or adding dormers on upper floors.

realistic view both of how much money you have available to spend and of how much you can call on in the way of raising additional cash if your budget doesn't cover all the work you want to do. In any budget there is considerable choice about where you can allocate your resources and where you can make significant savings by shopping around. Having a clear idea of the total fund before you begin will stop you losing your way.

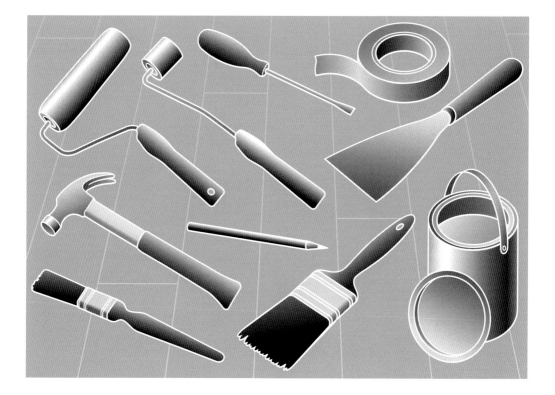

Above Poorly executed decoration is a major turn-off for potential buyers as it is difficult for them to see past the work they may have to do. It is important to invest in the correct tools and materials for each task and pay attention to detail.

It is important that once you have set a realistic budget you stick to it. If you spend so much that the added value covers only what you have spent, you will have no profit to propel you into buying a more expensive property. The only benefit will be that the house will be done to your taste – but will it really have been worth all the effort?

You must make sure that each item on the specification you prepare with the architect or builder is individually costed. Then review the specification thoroughly and think about where you might be able to make savings. Remember that you will have to pay VAT on everything, including the builder's fees.

Managing the project

Realism and organization are the two key qualities needed to run a successful building project. Above all, you must be realistic about your knowledge of building work and how much you can do yourself. If you bite off more than you can chew, you can call in the builders halfway through, but this is always much more expensive than if you had asked them to undertake the project from the start.

Before you start, ask yourself if you have the interest in the work and dedication to the project to want to make the detailed decisions. You also need to ask if you have the time to give the commitment necessary to manage a project that will probably require organizing five or six different workmen to turn up on the right day with the right materials.

The other side of project management is sourcing and buying materials. This is time-consuming, because you have to research the market thoroughly if you are going to save substantial amounts of money. Even when you have decided what and where to buy, you can find that you end up having to go to a second supplier for some parts that the first one doesn't have in stock. Project management is not something that can be done in your lunch hour, and delays are costly and have knock-on implications. One delay can easily lead to a three-month project developing into a nine-month one.

Be realistic

If you have any doubts about your capabilities or if the time you can spend on the project is limited, consider appointing an architect or a

---

Saving money

- Shop around for materials and make full use of the Internet. Negotiate hard with suppliers and ask for discounts if you are buying more than one of anything.
- Don't overspend on kitchen and bathroom fittings. All carcasses are made of MDF and only the doors and hinges vary in quality. Choose something from the basic ranges and change the handles to improve the look. National suppliers are not necessarily the cheapest, so check independent local retailers. Always make sure that the quality is appropriate to the value of the house. You will not significantly increase the value of a one-bedroom flat just because you install a mahogany bath panel.
- Flooring tiles and vinyl are cheaper than wooden laminates and last longer. Don't be afraid to use carpet where practical, which can also be cheaper.
- Avoid expensive paint brands. Many paint suppliers can match any colour in a cheaper, good-quality brand. Use paint rather than wallpaper.
- Recycle what is already in the house wherever possible. Sanitary fittings may be in need of a thorough clean and descaling. You can improve the appearance of ugly cupboards by changing the handles and adding decorative architraving and cornicing. Sand and fill rough walls rather than replastering them.

chartered building surveyor to act as your project manager. This will, of course, immediately add about another 10 per cent plus VAT to your bill, but it may still turn out to be the cheapest option.

You may decide that you want to project manage your own refurbishment even if you have used an architect to help you through the planning process. Apart from the time commitment, you will also need to get to grips with some of the technical aspects of the work so that you can supervise the builders effectively and see that the work is carried out in the proper order to ensure maximum speed and efficiency.

If you have no experience of this kind of work, you need to do some research into basic methods of construction, types of plumbing and heating systems, wiring and so on. There are a number of organizations that represent the building trades (see Useful Addresses, pages 193–200), which can give you advice on any aspect of your project. Most have websites, which are a fund of helpful information.

Employing a project manager

People undertaking house renovations are increasingly using project managers if they feel an architect is not required but do not have the time to supervise the building work closely themselves. A project manager will typically have a background in interior design and be experienced in managing ambitious remodelling projects; alternatively, they may be builders who have worked so closely with architects in the past that they can bring knowledge and experience of how to shape a project to your needs. They will

take charge of the overall management of a project, which should include hiring the builders, sourcing the materials and ensuring the project is completed on time and on budget.

Project managers are useful when you are renovating a flat and reorganizing rooms, and when you are short of time and cannot get away from work every day to meet the builders to make essential decisions. They can also get trade discounts on materials, which can be passed on. You should expect to pay around 10 per cent of the contract fee plus VAT to a project manager.

You should work with your project manager in much the same way as you would work with an architect (see page 68), discussing the project with them every day and making sure that you are consulted on as many as possible of the small decisions that will contribute to the overall finish of the property.

Using an architect

An architect will give advice on the design and structure of any alterations or extensions to your property, and given their specialized experience and expertise, they can often devise more elegant solutions than you could have thought of yourself. They are often particularly good at suggesting ways of manipulating the space in your house. Some of their best work can be seen not in grandiose buildings but in successful transformations of dank, ugly spaces into light-filled, spacious homes.

In addition to design work, an architect will handle the planning and building regulations applications. This is increasingly important. Some local authorities have become so

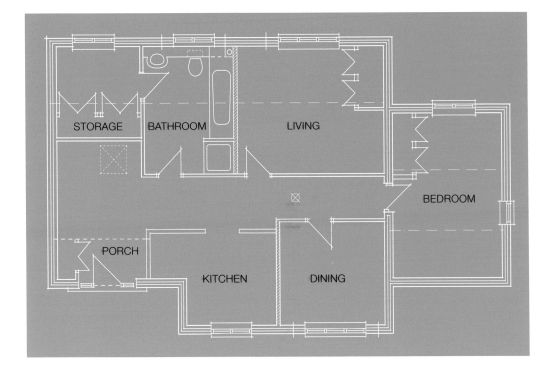

STORAGE   BATHROOM   LIVING

                                        BEDROOM

PORCH

        KITCHEN   DINING

bureaucratic on even modest alterations that loft conversions or side extensions sometimes have to go through four or five applications. This will apply particularly if what you are proposing sets a precedent for the street. For this reason, if you are proposing anything that needs planning permission, it is advisable to appoint an architect, even if you don't use one for managing the project.

If you are planning a renovation to a listed building, or one that is in a conservation area, you should probably appoint an architect. Regulations are much more stringent for these properties, both in terms of what you can do to them and the materials you can use. This is a specialist area, and it can prove to be expensive

Above If you are having work done by an architect, check the plans. Make sure that they follow your brief and ask for an explanation of anything that you do not understand or is not what you asked for. Think through whether your ideas work – changing your mind is much less expensive at this stage than after work has started.

if you inadvertently break the rules. It is therefore a good idea to appoint someone who has expertise in this field.

Any project where the cost of building is likely to exceed £150,000 should be undertaken with the supervision of an architect. The project is likely to be so complex that, unless you have professional help, you could easily come unstuck if you try to manage it yourself. Mistakes can become hugely expensive when this amount of money is involved.

You should use the architect throughout the project, from the earliest planning stage and initial contact with listed building or conservation officers, to planning and listed building applications, the preparation of the specification, researching the building firms you would like to tender, tendering, supervision of contract and tendering to sub-contractors, project management, and working with the quantity surveyor, structural engineer and other personnel. This will not shut you out from any involvement you want to have on the project, and it is helpful to the architect if you do work together, doing your own initial concept designs and detailed bathroom and kitchen designs, sourcing, researching suppliers and so on.

Establish a good working relationship

Many people have more trouble with architects than they do with builders. Most of these disputes relate to architects' costs, but a further frequently reported complaint is that architects' designs are impracticable for their clients' needs or are more concerned with the visual appearance of the property at the expense of how it will function.

Communication is the key to a successful relationship with your architect. This is why it is important to prepare your own brief before you meet a professional. You can then match their proposals against your brief and see how well they have sought to fulfil your criteria. You should also expect a detailed breakdown of the costs of the project at this stage.

The best way to build a successful relationship with an architect is to choose someone whose taste and style match yours, not just someone whose work and quality of work you like. When it comes to quick decisions, you need someone who will guess what you would like correctly. Be frank at every stage, and if you have concerns, voice them straightaway, as you would with any business project. Have the courage to admit you have changed your mind or don't like something that has been done, even if it seems too major to change or is likely to upset the team. The people you are paying to work with you want you to be pleased with the end result, even if there is a little grumbling along the way.

You need to liaise frequently with your architect while the project is under way – at times there should be almost daily telephone conversations. Renovation work on a large house may take one or two years to plan and execute, and to get value for money, you need to work together on every aspect of the design. Thrash issues out together, but from the beginning have a deal that you will work through the architect or there is no point in employing one.

The lines of command should be clearly defined so that there are no problems with 'he said this and she said that'. The architect's supervision should involve site meetings on a regular basis, and the architect should be responsible for checking the resulting action. If you go on regular site visits alone, note and discuss the progress, then call through any queries to the architect to follow them up. If everyone works as a team, there should be no falling out.

Go over drawings instantly and carefully – a scale ruler will be invaluable – and react swiftly to your architect. Feedback is vital to your architect. Keep the pressure on if things slow up. Push hard at the beginning to get the plans ready to submit for permission, because this is often a stage where architects delay since they know that the pressure will be on to get the job contracted once permissions are in place.

Double-check everything carefully as these plans will form the basis of a specification. Alterations after this will cost you both in your architect's time and in contract extras. Check the specifications as carefully as you are able to. Using different, even cheaper materials once the job is in progress will incur a cost for alteration of the specification.

Another common complaint about architects is that they are unwilling to work on projects costing less than £100,000. This may be true of many, particularly if their practice undertakes commercial as well as residential work, but local architects with smaller practices may be more approachable. As the housing market slows you may find architects are now more willing to undertake smaller projects than they were two or three years ago. If your project costs between £20,000 and £50,000 you might consider using a project manager (see page 66).

Choosing an architect

The best way to choose an architect is by word-of-mouth recommendation. There is no better source of information than a previous client who can tell you the strengths and weaknesses of the person you appoint.

The Royal Institute of British Architects (RIBA) offers a client advisory service, which enables you to specify what type of architect you are looking for – someone specializing in historic properties, in conversion of offices to residential and so on. If you are planning work on a listed building, some of the specialist housing groups, such as the Victorian Society or the Society for the Protection of Ancient Buildings, will be able to give you some advice.

It is a good idea to consider local people, but you should always take up references and contact more than one client. There are always shortcomings on any project, and you need to be in a position to assess whether the mistake was the fault of the architect or the client. Ask friends whose projects you like who they used, look at as much work as possible and speak to the local council.

If you are working on an old property, which involves getting permissions, you will need to establish regular contact with the listed building department and work with them, so this is a good place to start your search. Officially, they cannot make recommendations. Unofficially, they know who they like working with and respect, and this will be invaluable. Equally, you need to check that whomever you like actually manages to get permission for their proposals, because without a good relationship with planning and building regulators, an architect is ineffective.

When you have found someone who seems suitable, you need to find out how they work with builders and how builders see them. Builders hate some architects because they blame them for mistakes and leave them to shoulder the costs. The ideal is someone who is fair and reasonable, and good at working in a team with builders. Avoid an architect who suggests working with a particular builder – they should always be open to looking at a selection of suitable builders and giving a chosen few the chance to tender.

What do architects charge?

Most architects charge between 10 and 15 per cent of the value of the contract. Renovations are more expensive than new-build, and you will probably pay 15 per cent for such work. You will usually be asked for payment in stages. This should be done on a friendly basis, and you should ask to be given warning of when they will need another instalment. The 15 per cent should include much of the design work, but you can expect to pay extra if you revisit the designs substantially during the course of the project.

If the costs run out of control on a contract, which may happen if you are restoring an old building and there are structural or historic discoveries to contend with during the course of the work, you can ask the architect to take a sympathetic view of the extra costs. A good relationship will help here.

If you are only using an architect for the design element of a project, you should negotiate a fixed fee. This will probably be based on the architect's hourly rate, which can vary enormously depending on the individual practice. It is probably best to agree the fee upfront rather than letting hourly charges mount up inexorably. If the architect is out of pocket because the work has taken longer than expected, they will probably ask for an extra payment at the end.

Appointing a builder

The appointment of a builder is the critical decision for your peace of mind while a renovation project is under way. You have to find a builder who you are satisfied is competent to do the work, who will be reliable and not disappear on other jobs for weeks on end, and with whom you can establish a good working relationship so that you can meet the setbacks and iron out potential disagreements with good humour.

You need to find out if the builder has a reliable team of workmen with the different skills required to undertake the work at a steady pace. Building work can become slow and dispiriting if there is a two-week break while you wait for the plumber or electrician to become available to do their allotted task.

Word-of-mouth recommendation is always a good place to start because there is nothing more valuable than other people's experiences when it comes to finding out if a builder is reliable and satisfactory and can stick to the budget. Don't assume, however, that your friends' recommendations are a guarantee that there will be no trouble. The work you are undertaking might be different in scale from what they had done, and your friends' standards might not be as demanding as yours in terms of quality of finish. Always ask to look at their property to see and judge for yourself what has been done, and find out from them what problems they encountered.

The other way to find builders in the local area is to approach the estate agent who sold you the house. They can usually put you in touch with someone, although you will have to decide for yourself whether you trust the builder. Another alternative is to wander around local building sites, talk to some of the workmen and ask them to show you what they are doing. You can then get the telephone number of the head builder and take it from there.

Another approach is through the professional associations, such as the Federation of Master Builders, which maintain lists of members and make them available on request. A builder who applies to be a member goes through a vetting procedure to make sure that he meets basic standards of competence and can offer some financial stability. However, these are only basic standards, and membership is no guarantee of quality of work. Some professional organizations do offer an insurance scheme that will cover you in the event of a dispute or unfinished work, and it is worth considering this if you follow this route.

Scheduling the work

Before work begins you should prepare a renovation plan to determine the order and schedule of works. Discuss this schedule in detail with your builder and agree approximate timings as well as the order in which the work will be done. They will know what is likely to be realistic. Using the time schedule will allow you to plan when you need to buy your supplies.

When you are replacing a kitchen, for instance, it usually take about four weeks to get delivery of the new cupboards, so you need to get your order in early enough so that the builders are not held up.

A schedule of works should proceed in roughly the order summarized below.

Preparing a schedule The schedule for the work to be done should include the following main stages in this order.

Clearance This is the stage when everything that has to go from the property is demolished and removed, including kitchens, bathrooms, floor coverings, partition walls and old boilers. You will need a couple of strong workmen and a plumber if water services have to be capped off. This usually only takes two or three days depending on the extent of the work, but you will need a large skip for which you may need a permit from the local council.

Inspection The builder will now look over the property for unforeseen problems that you have not set out in the specification. This is the point at which you may discover hidden extras such as rising damp, woodworm and leaking pipes in ceilings from the flat above. Your contingency fund will be used to pay for this remedial work, and if you haven't got one, this is where your budget begins to come off the rails.

Construction This is the time when the builder begins the basic reconstruction work, such as moving walls and windows, digging out drains and laying new floors.

First fix The 'first fix' is the point at which the builder begins the rerouting of the services – for example, a new boiler and central-heating pipework will be installed but not connected up, and new wiring will go in, leaving the plasterer to conceal the wires in the walls.

Finishing The plasterer and decorators will render the walls and conceal all the new pipework and wires. The first coats of paint will be applied now so that places that are difficult to reach – behind radiators, for example – are covered at least once.

Second fix The 'second fix' is when the new sanitary fittings are installed and connected up. At this point, too, kitchen units and appliances go in. Sockets and light fittings are attached to the wiring. New flooring is laid and any tiling done in the kitchen and bathroom.

Decorating The final stage is decorating, when the painters apply top coats. The finishing touches, such as towel rails, mirrors and decorative glass, are also fitted at this stage.

Avoiding common problems

The best organized projects come unstuck. Being aware of the most usual reasons for things to go wrong may help you avoid them.

Delays

Builders usually have several projects running at the same time. As a consequence, they can get diverted away from your job, and this is the cause of many delays. You can minimize the risk of this happening in your contract by stipulating that payment will be forthcoming only at set stages of completion and imposing penalties for late completion of work.

Weather and sickness may cause delays that are not the builder's fault. If you plan your building work for the spring and summer, you can prevent some of the worst of the weather-related delays, but never underestimate the capacity of the British climate to spring a surprise.

Materials

The non-arrival of materials often holds up work. This is where you will find that you spend a great deal of time chasing alternative suppliers to arrange faster delivery. Remember to schedule enough lead-time for goods that take several weeks to be delivered.

Hidden work

Unexpected additions to the specification sometimes arise in the course of the job, either as a result of unseen problems becoming apparent or because you change your mind as the work goes on. The greater the preparation before you start, the less you should suffer from hidden extras, but they are part of any building job and you should be prepared. Changing your mind is not to be recommended, because you will pile on the additional costs for the extra time the work will take and the delay this could cause to other parts of the project. On the other hand, you only have the builders in once, so you might as well get it right.

Management

If you are in charge of managing the project, you have to keep up with events on a daily basis.

The builder's priority is to get the work done. If items in your specification cannot be found easily, you might find that they are liable to use any available alternative in order to keep the project on track.

Be prepared to stand your ground and argue the toss over each individual point until you drive yourself mad, let alone the builder. Getting the fine detail right is essential to the finish of a project – and that is where the enhanced value lies.

Getting planning permission

The planning system is designed to protect the environment and public interest in preserving the character and amenities of an area. The main responsibility for administration lies with the local authority. How they interpret the law varies widely, and alterations that go through on the nod, say, in one area may take three appeals in another.

The planning officers pay attention to how well designed a building is and how it will look after the work is finished. This can make it difficult to obtain permission for contemporary designs in areas rich in period houses, and planners tend to lag behind architects in recognizing imaginative solutions for difficult conversions. This can make the system frustrating, and you should never buy a property for which you are planning radical changes without first consulting an architect with in-depth experience of dealing with the local authority about the council's attitude to such proposals.

As a rule the kind of projects that require planning permission will include:

- Changing the exterior appearance of a building.
- Creating or reducing light.
- Building a separate house or large shed in your garden.
- Splitting a house into flats.
- Increasing the size of your house by more than 10 per cent.
- Extending the house above the current roof.
- Changing the use from residential to commercial.
- Building something that goes against the terms of the original planning consent.
- Building an extension that might obstruct the view of road users or involve new access to a major road.

There are more stringent rules for building and renovating work undertaken on properties that are listed (see page 74) and for those in an Area of Outstanding Natural Beauty, a conservation area, a national park and those in the Norfolk and Suffolk Broads. There will be tighter restrictions on external changes because they affect the appearance of the house in a protected environment.

If you are in doubt about any planning permission issues, you should consult your local planning authority for advice. Do not under any circumstances proceed without planning permission if you need it. Your neighbours are bound to notice and will telephone the council to check that the work is legal. If you are in breach of any of the many different regulations, a council has the power to make you tear down all the work and restore the property to its original state at your own expense.

Work on a flat may also require consent from the freeholder, so check the details of your lease before you begin any work.

Submitting an application

Contact the planning department of your local council, and they will explain the process to you. Once you have applied, a notice will be posted outside the property to ask for comments from neighbours who might have valid objections if their light will be affected or if they are concerned that the new work will be an eyesore. You will have to pay a fee for an extension, which is calculated by the area of the new floor, at a rate of £220 per 0.1 hectare.

It usually takes about eight weeks for permission to come through. If your application is rejected, take the trouble to find out why and prepare to resubmit it with some key changes to take account of objections.

Other consents

Other consents may be required even if you do not need planning permission. If you live in a listed building you may need listed building consent (see right), and in a conservation area you may need conservation area consent. These regulations can govern the internal alterations you are allowed to make and the materials deemed suitable for use in the property. These regulations are getting tighter – knocking through rooms in a Victorian house, for instance, is more restricted than it was 10 years ago.

Even quite simple building works may require building regulation consent. Check with the building control department of your local authority. These controls regulate the quality of the building work and the technical aspects of the work. They come into play once the building work has started and are designed to ensure that your work complies with fire regulations, sanitation requirements and means of escape from upper stories. In London demolition and rebuilding of external or party walls is also covered, where you may have to pay for a surveyor acting for your neighbour before you start any such work to prevent disputes further down the line.

The district surveyor will carry out inspections of the building work as it progresses, and fees must be paid for this.

Restoring a listed building

Owning a listed building usually means you have the privilege of living in a beautiful property, but with it comes a burden of additional regulation and legal requirements. Complying with these puts up the cost of maintenance, sometimes substantially, so you should be aware of what you may be letting yourself in for if you decide to buy a listed property.

Your property is categorized as listed if it appears on the statutory list compiled by the Department of Culture, Media and Sports, and at present in England alone there are about 500,000 such buildings. Nearly all buildings built before 1700 and most built between 1700 and 1840 are listed. When it comes to buildings dating from after 1840, listing will depend on architectural quality or technical innovation, the significance of the architect or other historical associations. A local authority search will show if a building is listed.

The grades for listing buildings

- **Grade I:** buildings of exceptional interest
- **Grade II:** particularly important buildings of more than special interest
- **Grade III:** buildings of special interest, warranting every effort to preserve them

All of a listed building is listed – inside and outside. There is no such thing as a listed façade. Anything fixed to a listed building is also listed. Any demolition, alteration or extension of a listed building that would affect its character requires listed building consent. They may also require planning permission. It is an offence to carry out work without these consents. You should always approach your local council for advice if you are in doubt, because the penalties can be severe.

Repairs and restoration that affect the character of a listed building will also require listed building consent. The authorities prefer to see repair and renovation of original materials rather than their replacement but this is often more expensive.

Owners of listed buildings are regarded as the custodians of the nation's architectural heritage and have a responsibility to keep them in good repair. If an owner neglects a listed building, the local authority can require specific repairs to be carried out. If the building is unoccupied, the council may undertake the work itself and bill the owner for the costs

incurred. If the owner fails to carry out any specific repairs, the council can issue a compulsory purchase order.

One bonus of owning a listed building is that some alteration work on certain types of buildings enjoys a zero rate of VAT, but this does not apply to routine repair and maintenance.

In addition to listed buildings, local authorities designate conservation areas where it considers that an area has special architectural or historic interest, which it is desirable to preserve. Although the regulations are not as draconian as for listed buildings, you will still be required to obtain consent for certain works that normally do not need permission.

If you own a house in a conservation area, you will need to obtain consent for the demolition of any part of the building, including shop fronts and front boundary walls. Planning permission is also required if you want to render existing brickwork, alter or extend the roof or install a satellite dish. These controls are designed to protect the environment of the area.

Obtaining grants

It is worth exploring whether you can claim a grant towards the cost of renovating a house. Although they are increasingly difficult to obtain, some properties, especially listed buildings, will attract a grant.

Local authority house renovation grants

Grants for renovating old houses used to be the route for enterprising young couples to get started on the housing ladder. They could buy an old house and install basic sanitation and modern facilities for the first time. Now they have disappeared, as local authorities no longer have huge budgets to spend on housing.

New schemes are available to help improve private housing that has fallen into disrepair, however. They are mostly for home owners on low incomes or the elderly, but all owner-occupiers are eligible. In addition to grants, there are also low-cost loans and equity release schemes. Each local authority is free to decide how to award financial assistance, so the best place to start is by contacting your local council. Grants may be available, for instance, to replace a defective damp-proof course or old wiring.

English Heritage

If you own a listed building, specifically those listed Grade I or Grade II, you may be eligible for a grant from English Heritage, which provides funds for the repair and conservation of historic buildings. Priority goes to buildings at risk, private homes that have been in the same family for more than 30 years and where a grant will bring social and economic benefits. Grants are not available for new owners, although if you have a farm and there are redundant barns or outbuildings, these might be eligible.

Charities

If you have a listed building in need of urgent repairs you may be able to get a small contribution from preservation organizations, such as the Society for the Protection of Ancient Buildings and the Victorian Society, but you would have to make a good case to show that you deserve help and that the money is unlikely to cover much of the cost of repairs.

Energy-saving grants

Other bodies offering grants for home improvements are largely given to improve the use of energy. These focus on installing insulation to reduce consumption and generating renewable energy for domestic heating and electricity. The Energy Saving Trust encourages the use of alternative forms of energy and offers grants to help home owners install solar power. Specifically this covers photovoltaic systems, or solar PV systems, which are connected to the national grid. They generate electricity from sunlight to power ordinary household appliances, such as PCs and lights. They are not cheap to install, costing about £12,000 for a house. The grant covers up to 50 per cent of the cost, and the work has to be done by an accredited installer. Your eligibility for a grant will be means tested and will also depend on the regional power supplier. Advice is available from the Energy Saving Trust's network of advice centres.

The Clear Skies scheme, run by the Building Research Establishment, encourages home owners to use renewable energy systems, from solar thermal hot-water devices to wood-burning stoves. Home owners can receive grants ranging from £500 to £5,000.

Although your heating bills will fall as a result of this work, the payback time is long, perhaps as much as 10 years. There is no way of assessing the improved value of a house that is partly able to generate its own energy, but environmentalists think it is well worth doing in any case.

Summary: Planning the Renovation

- Be clear about your objectives before appointing a builder.
- Prepare a thorough brief listing all work needed as well as everything you would like to do. See page 63 for a checklist.
- Set a budget. Make it as realistic as possible and stick to it. Cost every item on the specification, include a contingency fund and VAT. Explore obtaining a grant.
- Enhanced value lies in getting the detail right.
- Be realistic about your ability to manage the project yourself. Delays cost and have knock-on implications.
- A project manager can hire builders, source materials and ensure that a project is finished on time and on budget.

Architects and builders
- Use an architect if what you propose needs planning permission, if the building is listed or in a conservation area and where costs are likely to exceed £150,000.
- Expect to pay an architect 10–15 per cent of the value of the contract. Negotiate a fixed fee if they are undertaking design work only.
- Word-of-mouth is the best recommendation. Take up references and contact more than one client.
- Agree a schedule. Planning and scheduling are crucial to ensure that everything is done in the right order.

- Delays, materials, hidden work and management are the cause of most problems.

Permissions and consents
- If unsure of what consents you need, consult your local planning authority.
- Do not proceed without planning permission if you need it. It usually takes about eight weeks to be processed.
- Listed buildings are subject to additional regulation and legal requirements. It is an offence to carry out work without listed building consent and planning permission.

⑧ Creating Space

The internal layout of a property is one of the most important factors in determining its value. Buyers will pay a premium if the arrangement of the rooms exactly meets their needs and, more importantly, if the property feels right as they make that all-important first viewing. Changing a layout is not that difficult and is a sure way of adding value.

The rules of layout

The wrong layout means that a property is fundamentally flawed. Buyers may register this only subliminally, but the negative reaction will be strong enough to deter them from making an offer. A badly laid-out property, whether modernized or unmodernized, can be bought for a bargain price, and reorganizing the space is one of the best ways of making a profit. Even properties newly refurbished by developers can linger on the market for months because the owner has paid insufficient attention to some basic rules.

The rules of layout are simple. The private and public zones in a house should be clearly defined and separated, but at the same time there should be sufficient flexibility in the use of rooms to allow buyers to adapt the house or flat to their own needs. A house should also appear to have been designed to facilitate ease of lifestyle because we live in an age when everyone is short of time. A large kitchen, where people can also eat, is, therefore, near the top of everyone's priorities. After the kitchen, people want a certain number of bedrooms and a certain number of living rooms.

Adding value through redesign

When you are planning to do up a house, think first about how to reorganize the space in the house. Look at each room individually – its light sources, its aspect and outlook – and consider if and how these could be changed. Assess how the house could be opened up in terms of height and volume. Introducing different levels, such as mezzanines and galleries, can spill light throughout the whole building and give a feeling of spaciousness to even quite restricted spaces.

You will have to strive to create a balance between openness and privacy, and this balance will vary according to the type of property. Open-plan living is popular in all age groups, but young couples tend to sell their loft spaces and move to conventional terraced houses when children arrive. This is because privacy within the home becomes more important at that stage of their lives.

A remodelling project will involve major decisions, such as whether to demolish the back extension and rebuild it, and minor ones, such as the colour of paint on the wall. The structural and technical problems of a building are fairly easy to identify, but the functional and aesthetic issues may not be so simple to define. There may be more than one way to solve the problems involved.

Practical considerations

As you think about possible ways to achieve better use of space in your house, draw up a list of possibilities and consider each in terms of cost, feasibility and appropriateness for the property. Although you need to find solutions for

Example

When he was working on a three-storey Victorian house in a smart suburb, the developer was so anxious to cram in four bedrooms that he put two in the basement and two on the first floor. The kitchen, which could have been large and spacious if it had been located in the basement, was instead jammed into a narrow extension at the back of the property. This left the house unsold for months. Families with children do not want them sleeping two floors away, down in the basement, which is the most vulnerable floor to break-ins. Childless couples, who do not want or need a four-bedroom house, would have preferred a better kitchen and more reception space. There were no takers for this house, even though another one in the same street with a better layout went under offer within 10 days with an asking price that was 15 per cent higher.

each specific area of the house, you should avoid piecemeal alterations because the house may lose a sense of integrity and wholeness.

The best solution is the one that solves most problems. If you have to undertake a structural repair, it is an ideal opportunity to combine it with an aesthetic or functional improvement. You may be limited in reorganizing layout by the existing structure – moving a staircase or altering the drainage is expensive – and to some extent you have to work with what you have. There are also some features that cannot or should not be removed or altered – period fireplaces and wooden panelling, for example, or the appearance of the front of the house (unless you are restoring a house with stone cladding to its original appearance).

Moving walls to create larger or smaller rooms is in the majority of circumstances relatively easy. Similarly, look at the access to every room in the house and how the circulation around the house could be improved. You do not want a house in which you have to go through one room to get to another, unless it is an *en suite* bathroom.

Consider the views from the property. If you enjoy a fine focal point, think about how you might rearrange the house to draw the eye towards it. If you have an attractive garden you might be able to install large windows or double doors for access to the back rather than through the traditional Victorian side door. This has the effect of bringing the outside in and filling the house with light.

In practice, there are a number of layouts that should be avoided but are still often found. Bathrooms should not be downstairs next to the kitchen; this is a hangover from the Victorian layout when there was only an external WC. Any awkwardly shaped rooms should be altered to create a sense of each room being an integral whole in itself.

Enhancing existing space

Making better use of the existing space is generally the cheapest option and often involves no structural work at all.

> ## Overcoming space restrictions
>
> There are four main ways in which you can improve the available space in a house:
>
> - Enhance the existing space
> - Rearrange the existing space
> - Convert unused space
> - Add new space

You should consider the layout of the furniture and how it might impede the best use of space in a room. Are your storage cupboards adequate? Putting away clutter will immediately make a room look bigger. Think about the vertical use of shelving to increase storage. However, do not cram every spare space or fill the hallways and landings with bookshelves and storage cupboards, because this can make the property look small and overcrowded. Spare space helps lend a feeling of harmony to the house and allows the residents time to breathe.

Painting a room a lighter colour will also make it look larger, and improved lighting will brighten its appearance.

Relatively minor alterations, such as moving a door, can also help improve existing space by allowing a better flow of traffic through the room.

Rearranging space

If altering the use of a room does not solve your problem, consider extending it. Moving a wall allows you to change an awkwardly shaped room and improve its proportions. Many interwar houses, for instance, were built with small bathrooms and a separate WC next door. Knocking down the wall between the two and taking additional space from the hallway, if it is available, can greatly enlarge your bathroom, and can increase the value of your home, particularly if you have a separate WC elsewhere in the house.

Similarly, if you have an overlarge room, you can divide it by erecting a partition wall or a room divider, such as glass bricks or bookcases. Arranging the furniture into clearly defined spaces will also contribute to the feeling of a room with separate functions.

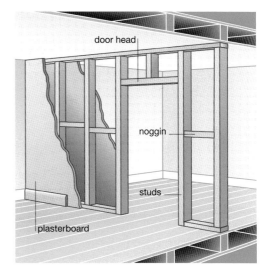

Converting unused space

Unused space is typically found in attics or basements and sometimes in garages. It is cheaper to extend upwards and downwards rather than to build outwards because the necessary foundations are already in place. It may also be the only available option in towns where space is at a premium and planning regulations do not allow you to increase the footprint of your house.

A loft extension may involve raising the roof, although sometimes there is enough usable space in the existing roof void. Basements require patient attention to damp-proofing and to ways of increasing natural light. Garages can be demolished and a side extension built in its place, although this will require planning permission. Some repairs and alterations to the exterior may be required as a result of the work, but these formerly dank and gloomy holes can become attractive living quarters.

Above If dividing a large room into two, a stud wall is a practical option if it is not to be a load-bearing structure. It is attached to the floor, ceiling and walls and then plasterboard is attached. Ensure that the layout is practical; having two small rooms rather than one large one may not add as much value as you think, especially if accessing one via the other will be awkward.

Adding new space

Parkinson's law applies to space in houses as much as to time and work. No matter how big your house is, you will expand to fill all available space as you accumulate possessions. Above all, the arrival of children will force changes on a household, and as they grow they require more and more space for their toys and belongings. Moving house may not be the only solution. If the main living areas of your house are well laid out and suit your needs but you now require extra bedrooms or a playroom for children or a study, you should consider making additional space, usually by extending at the back or side and taking space from the garden.

Large one- and two-storey extensions will need new foundations, exterior walls, roofing and full utility services. This is the point at which you call in an architect. You will need planning permission and a full specification to put the work out to tender with several builders. Be prepared for months of disruption and dirt. Depending on the size of the job, you may even have to move into rented accommodation while the work is under way, and this can sometimes be cheaper because the builders can work more quickly if they do not have to clean up and make the house habitable before they pack up in the evening.

In terms of adding value you must make sure that the property remains balanced when you are extending or converting. Normally, adding square footage should increase the value of your property, but it won't work if the property becomes top- or bottom-heavy. Three- or four-storey Victorian houses can become too tall and narrow and appear to be all stairs if they are overextended. On the other hand, if the extension provides additional space for bathrooms, restoring one of the bedrooms to its original use, this will undoubtedly add value. You should, in any case, aim to get back the money you spend on the conversion in the property's increased value.

Planning considerations

When you are planning a conversion, analyse the existing space you have in terms of the following features.

Headroom You must provide the necessary ceiling height to comply with planning consents as well as ensuring that the room is comfortable for your use. The minimum height you need is 2.3m (7ft 6in), but 2.4m (8ft) is better.

Daylight and air Without daylight and air rooms cannot be regarded as habitable. If you cannot introduce sufficient of either, you should think only in terms of installing bathrooms and utility rooms. As a rule, the glazing area of windows for a habitable space should be 10 per cent of the usable floor area, and half of that should be suitable for ventilation.

Circulation Consider what access is necessary, the type of staircase you want as well as its proximity to the hall or outside doors and how the converted space will tie into the rest of the property.

Zoning A house works best if it divides naturally into those rooms with an esentially public function, such as reception rooms for

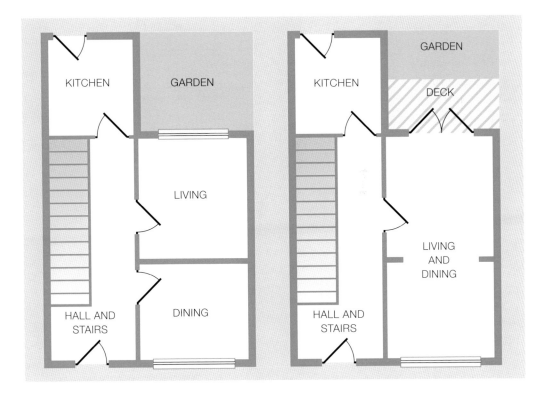

entertaining, and private areas, such as bedrooms. You will need to consider how the converted space will fit in relative to the zones of the house and the other use of space.

Utilities It is important to assess what services will have to be provided in the planned new space. Electricity and heating are essential, but you may also require plumbing and air conditioning.

Weatherproofing Consider whether the existing space needs to be insulated or sealed with tanking or a damp-proof course to protect it against the elements.

Above Most Victorian terraced houses were built with separate front and back rooms. Removing the dividing wall to make full use of the space is a well-established means of adding value to such a house because the different layout is more suited to modern living. By changing the window in the back room to patio doors, this also makes use of what was a neglected part of the garden.

Pros and cons of loft and basement conversions

Loft/Basement	Pros	Cons
Loft	Usually cheaper to extend up then down or outwards; can install skylights to introduce natural daylight and ventilation; new rooms better suited to use as bedrooms.	Almost always need planning permission; staircase will eat into valuable living space on floor below; may not have the required headroom for expansion.
Basement	Less likely to need planning permission; can be designed as self-contained flat with separate access.	Can be prohibitively expensive; raises concerns with damp, ventilation and natural daylight.

Exterior changes New windows may be necessary, and this may require planning permission. The windows will have to be in keeping with the rest of the house, at least at the front.

Loft conversions

Converting the loft into usable living space is one of the most popular ways of gaining additional space. The conversion usually provides one or more additional bedrooms and bathrooms, but the space can sometimes be adapted for use for working from home. It is best to keep this area as part of the private zone of the house, because you do not want visitors having to climb through the rest of the house to reach it.

Headroom

The first consideration in a loft extension is headroom. Assess whether the roof was built using trussed rafters or purlins. The latter type is much easier to convert into usable loft space but is usually found only in houses built before 1965. If your roof has a low pitch or is framed with trusses, you may have to raise the entire roof to gain additional space. While this adds considerably to the cost of the project, it does ensure that sloping eaves and wasted space in the corners are kept to a minimum. When you are calculating the headroom height, remember that you are likely to have to strengthen the floor and this may absorb up to 15cm (6in) of space, so include that figure in your calculations.

Windows and light

If your roof will give enough headroom – at least 50 per cent of the space should be 2.4m (8ft) high – you may be able to install Velux skylights or dormer windows to increase your space and natural light. A dormer window will add visual interest to the room, enhance the view and the external appearance of the property.

Left Expanding a property by converting the loft into a bedroom or office is a popular way of adding value. Although they are not appropriate for older buildings, Velux windows are a good way of introducing light, because, unlike dormer windows, they sit almost flush with the roof and all the light gets in.

Access

Next consider how you will get to the new floor. Where are you going to locate the staircase and what type of staircase are you going to install? Ideally, the staircase should run from the landing rather than from a bedroom, and if your current loft access is from a bedroom, you will need to consider relocating the entry point. If the loft is to be used primarily for storage, a spiral staircase or ladder staircase will be suitable, especially as these take up less space than a standard staircase. Any conversion that is designed to provide extra family accommodation should have a standard staircase, for both safety and fire protection purposes.

Staircases can take up a lot of room, and you need to consider how the loss of space on the lower level might affect the value of your property. If there is a serious problem one solution might be to install an external staircase from the ground floor at the back of the property and glaze it over. This can also double as a fire escape, which will, in any case, be required in buildings above five storeys in height.

Insulation

Insulation is critical in a loft extension, especially if you have raised the roof and lost the existing insulation. Without adequate insulation, the rooms will get hot in summer and cold in winter. You will also need to insulate the floor, for both sound- and fire-proofing.

Structure

A major consideration is whether the additional load of a loft conversion will place a significant extra strain on the existing structure. You may have to reinforce the building, and in these circumstances you will need to take advice from a structural engineer.

Permissions

Loft extensions often – but not always – need planning permission. Building regulation approval and party wall consents from adjoining properties, if applicable, cannot be ignored, and it is probably advisable to use an architect to design a suitable structure. You may find that the weight of the new walls on the existing structure and foundations may cause problems.

Planning permission may not always be available. If you own a listed building or a house in a designated conservation area, you may find that rules on the streetscape do not allow extensions. In any area you are unlikely to be able to raise the roof height above those of neighbouring properties, but precedent is frequently all important in planning approvals, so check what other extensions have been done in the street.

Costs

The cost of a loft conversion will depend on the size of the project and whether you have to raise the roof. Even on a small conversion you are unlikely to spend less than £30,000, and £50,000 may be more realistic, while for large houses the sums could well run up to £100,000. You may find that although you get your money back in terms of the increased value of the property, you will not make a profit. You should discuss valuations with a local estate agent before you begin work.

Basement conversions

Basements have a bad reputation among house buyers. Beset with damp problems and blighted by low ceilings and poor natural light, they tend to get used as a useful place to store junk that might be better sent to the tip. However, the high costs of moving and the pressure on space in cities has led to a renewed interest in how this space can be used more effectively.

The uses to which a converted basement can be put to are legion. It can be a self-contained flat for an au pair or nanny, later offering a den for teenage or student children and possibly even a buy-to-let investment (although tenants tend not to like living in the same property as the landlord).

Separation

The key decision is whether to keep the staircase leading to the upper parts of the house. If it is removed it creates a better flat in the basement but will make it more expensive to return the flat to the main part of the house, should that become necessary later on.

You also have to decide whether to keep the utilities as one with the rest of the house or separate them. If you are planning to let the space, it may be wise to install separate utilities.

There are financial implications in creating a self-contained flat out of your basement. As a separate dwelling it may be liable for capital gains tax if it is later sold. It will also be subject to independent council tax, and you will not be eligible for the tax allowance provided under the government's rent-a-room scheme. You will, however, be able to offset expenses against the tax due on rental income, as it will be deemed a commercial let.

Headroom

If you do not have full-height ceilings in the basement, you will have to excavate the floor to give you the extra headroom, and not every house is suitable for this type of work. You need to take care that you will not hit the drains running below the house, and it will be expensive to move them. In addition, you should not dig out below the foundation level, because this will damage the structural safety of the house. This is easy to do in old houses, where foundations are more or less non-existent.

If the house is built on sand, you will find the costs of digging out prohibitive because you will effectively be underpinning your house, that is, building new and deeper foundations. Houses built after the Second World War rarely had cellars, and houses built before 1850 had little in the way of foundations, making excavation work potentially dangerous.

Windows and light

If the basement has no windows, the space may still be usable as a recreation room, a home cinema or media centre, a workshop or laundry room. Artificial lighting and mechanical ventilation become important in these cases. Low-voltage halogen lighting is the most suitable because it is bright enough to create a daylight effect in the gloomiest of surroundings.

Access

If you decide to keep the staircase from the ground floor, consider its suitability for taking a much heavier load of family traffic than when the area was the cellar. Victorians were notoriously mean in providing adequate staircases to cellars and lofts, and some are little better than fixed ladders and far too steep for you or your children to run up and down with ease. You may need to put in a much sturdier staircase to ensure proper ease of access and to improve the appearance.

Damp

Damp is the bugbear of all who live in basements, and with the water table rising in many parts of the country, the problem is likely to get worse. Any problems must be corrected at the start of the conversion work. Chemical damp-proof courses and tanking if a wall abuts the ground – as happens with houses built on hills or set below a road – will provide a seal. The biggest cause of damp is, however, not rising damp from the ground but condensation from inadequate ventilation. If air circulation is restricted by lack of windows, you should consider installing and using extractor fans. Airbricks above ground are another good way to increase the airflow.

Another cause of damp in basements is surface water on the ground leaking through. You should check that all the down pipes from the roof are channelled away from the walls into a gully to drain away. Check that patios have not been laid above the damp-proof level, which happens quite often as people resurface their patios without taking up the old tiles or bricks, raising the new surface too high. If there are persistent problems with water seepage, the earth around the walls should be excavated, the walls waterproofed from the outside and proper drainage installed.

If the signs of damp on the walls point to only minor seepage, some builders will recommend the use of masonry paint or paints specially prepared to block damp. These are at best only a temporary solution, and you will probably do better to spend the time and money fixing the original cause of the damp. If you are selling the property, it is better to be honest about the problem of damp because surveyors use meters that register any moisture in the walls and will recommend remedial action accordingly.

Floors

If the basement floor is dry it is suitable for a number of floor coverings, such as wood, tiles or carpets. In many old houses, however, the original earth floor often still lies below the wooden floorboards and joists. In such circumstances, you need to install a new concrete slab, lined with plastic sheeting below, to prevent water penetration. You can then lay your floor covering on top. Cork tiles and linoleum are not the best choice for laying on concrete, and you should always use more robust materials.

Costs

Basement conversion work is not cheap. You should think in terms of spending around £100,000 to convert your basement, and it is probably not worth the effort in terms of adding value unless your house is worth more than £750,000. However, in cities where family houses are in short supply and space is at a premium, it is worth considering even if your property is worth less.

Back extensions

In terraced Victorian and Edwardian houses the most usual way to alter and increase space is at the back of the house. These houses often boast long, narrow extensions, which were originally built as single- or double-storey structures to provide the kitchen and scullery and, above, an extra bedroom. You will probably have to live with whatever height exists, because planning departments are increasingly reluctant to allow additional storeys to be built at the back because of loss of light for the neighbours.

Many of these houses have come up for renovation over the last 30 years, and it has long been the practice to knock the original kitchen and scullery together to make one large room and then extend outwards. The drawback is that little thought was given to the appearance of these new extensions, and they were frequently erected with flat roofs. Nearing the end of their lives, these lean-to extensions actually detract value from the property, because they are so ugly. It is worth considering knocking it down and rebuilding any such extensions to a higher standard with a pitched roof, which will add considerable value and appeal to your house.

In houses from the same period that were originally too small to merit a back extension, developers usually built one later to house the kitchen and bathroom. The disadvantages of this type of extension are that it takes a sizeable lump out of what is an already small town garden and leaves you with a dark, gloomy and narrow outside passage to the garden, often called the 'dogleg'.

Making the most of a 'dogleg'

If you buy a property with a narrow, uninspiring dogleg, you have a number of options to improve it, ranging from the cheap to the seriously expensive. At the outset you have to decide whether you want the space to be incorporated into the house or into the garden. Look where the light falls at the back of the house. If your dogleg is a sun trap, you may be better leaving it as outside space, which can be used for, say, maintenance work, and to improve ventilation to the back reception room.

The cheap option is to turn the dogleg into the link to the garden, giving access through improved glazed doors from the living room. You may have to replace a window with doors in this room, but this will enhance the natural light in a part of the house that is often dark. You will gain improved views of the garden from the house, which will make it more attractive. Install good-quality paving and suitable plants to scramble up the side walls, and you have made the area instantly more attractive.

A second, more expensive option is to turn the area into a conservatory. This is only a good idea if the area benefits from sunlight, and remember that a plastic conservatory, such as those found in DIY shops, does not add value to a Victorian house because it detracts from the appearance of the property. But it can be an attractive option in a more modern property.

The most expensive option and the one that will create substantial added value is to extend the side wall of the house outwards to include the dogleg. You will need to put in a glazed roof and doors the full width of the house to improve the natural light in the original, now middle,

Above A simple, all-glass conservatory suits modern-style homes and can make a play area for children or a space for dining. When considering adding a conservatory, it is best to check with the local planning office or an architect whether you need to get planning permission and that your plans comply with building regulations.

Above Conservatories are available in a wide range of sizes, styles and prices. Always suit the style of the conservatory to the house: a traditional Edwardian timber, for example, will suit an older home, while a modern metal and plastic one would not.

room. In effect, this creates a modern half to a period house, which will become the heart of the family home for cooking, children's homework and dining. Because it is at the back of the house, planners are more relaxed that the modern appearance will not detract from the period style of the street at the front.

The extensive use of glass to ensure the back reception room does not lose light helps to dissolve the boundaries between the kitchen and the garden, and the extra light can flow right through the hall to the front door. The union of interior and exterior space, if properly done, is enormously appealing, creating the impression that the garden is an outdoor room for the summer months.

Extensions do not need to blend in with the original property to look appealing. A modern extension can help to preserve the architectural integrity of the house better than a reproduction period conservatory, but it should, nonetheless, appear to be a main part of the house as far as possible, not an afterthought that divides the property into two parts.

Costs

You will need to think of spending at least £50,000. The work will involve excavating and opening up walls. It is time-consuming work because the builders have to carry the materials to the back of the property, something that will be reflected in their estimates, and you also have to pay VAT on extensions. But, depending on how stylish the addition looks once it is complete, you can usually add several times what you have spent to the value of your property.

Garage conversions

If you do not need your garage for storing a car you can convert it into usable living space at only a moderate cost (see also page 81). The structure is essentially complete, and if the garage is attached to the house, the utilities are nearby. Assuming the walls and roof are in good condition, you will only need small structural modifications, such as installing new windows and closing the existing garage doorway. Other work will involve insulation and the finishing of the floor, walls and ceiling. If the walls are not sturdy enough, you may have to consider underpinning, and this may be worth doing only if you really need the space, but you are unlikely to recover the cost in the increased value of the house.

Garages are large, open spaces, so they are especially suitable for conversion to studios or offices or a family playroom. It may be desirable to install glazed doors leading to the garden to connect the space with an outdoor living area.

Garage floors are usually concrete slabs and consequently hard underfoot. You should consider laying a wooden floor on top to soften the impact rather than just carpet. If there is sufficient headroom you could install joists and floorboards and even lay underfloor heating and plumbing services if needed. This will save you the cost of excavating the floor for pipework.

Converted garages are unlikely to add much value to the property simply because they look exactly what they are: a converted garage or cheap extension. In some parts of the country secure parking space is at such a premium that you may gain more value from keeping the space as a garage.

Porch conversions

A porch that is little used or is just a convenient place to leave a shopping trolley, pushchairs and bicycles can be enclosed and finished to expand an existing room in the house. This probably works better at the back of the house than at the front, where the appearance on the street has to be taken into account. It works well off a kitchen, for instance, where it can become an adjacent laundry room or a sunroom. If it is large enough it can even become a study or child's playroom.

As with a garage, the existing structure of foundation, floors and roof is already in place. Again, these must be checked to see if they are adequate for a conversion. The use of the space should be compatible with adjacent rooms, and the conversion should not detract from the natural daylight in the existing rooms.

Any value added from a conversion will depend on the overall size of the property. The value of a small ground-floor flat that gains extra space in this way could increase by 5–10 per cent if the new room can be counted as a study or even a small playroom or just a useful additional room. In a house the gain will be minimal, and the work is worth doing only if it enhances your enjoyment of the property.

Building a conservatory

In a recent survey by the Halifax 51 per cent of home-owners said a conservatory was their most desired luxury. In reality, conservatories add little to the value of a house unless your main sitting room is small and the space from an additional living area improves the accommodation. You should, however, get your money back as long as the work is well done. Conservatories that look like cheap extensions detract from a property's value.

Position

The direction in which your conservatory faces is critical, because this will determine when and how you use it. Although a south-facing structure is usually regarded as desirable because it gets the sun all year round, it can be roasting and unusable during the summer months. If the area you have designated for a conservatory is a suntrap, you might be better leaving it as an outdoor patio complete with external heaters so you can sit out as late as mid-autumn. In fact, a west-facing conservatory,

which will get afternoon and evening sun, is the most attractive position, while an east-facing one will get morning sun only. If the area gets little sun because it is on the north side or because of surrounding buildings, it isn't worth turning into a conservatory, as it will still be gloomy even under glass.

Style

If you are determined to go ahead it is important that the style you choose is in keeping with the age of your house and that it doesn't ruin the appearance or obstruct important access paths. Specialist conservatory builders can provide you with a full service, from design and siting to furnishings, such as the flooring and blinds. There are two main problems with conservatories. One is that after a time the roof will leak; the other is ensuring that the glass doors leading to the garden do not allow rainwater to come through, flooding the floor during a downpour. Much will depend on the competence of your builder, so choose the contractor carefully.

Permissions

You do not necessarily need planning permission to add a conservatory. It will depend on its size and where you want to put it, but check with your local authority. If you don't consult the planning department, your neighbours might when the work starts, and this will risk holding up your contractor, which costs money and is inconvenient. You will have to comply with energy-efficiency regulations, so special glass has to be used, and heating and ventilation are subject to certain criteria.

Costs

Although prices for a self-build conservatory start at £1,500, you should expect to spend between £10,000 and £20,000 if you are employing a company to design and erect it for you. The cost can rise to £50,000 depending on what you are trying to achieve.

Converting entire buildings

In some parts of Britain it is possible to buy properties that were originally designed for some other purpose and convert them to residential use. There is huge potential here, but before you buy, investigate the local authority's attitude to change of use.

Barns

The Home Counties of England are now dotted with luxury homes built out of once-utilitarian agricultural barns. Everything is considered suitable for conversion from cattle-sheds to piggeries. The advantages are obvious: there is a character building, rich in natural materials, especially wood, with soaring ceiling heights and scope for big, open-plan living areas on the ground floor in a rural setting.

The fashion for barn conversions started in the 1970s as large-scale farming practices rendered many 19th-century farm buildings redundant. Left derelict and falling into ruin, they became an eyesore, so planners were keen to encourage their conversion to residential use. A shortage of building land for development, combined with the inherent attraction of the buildings, led to a surge in demand. Buyers were given a fairly free hand in how they converted the buildings externally and internally.

In recent years planners have become more concerned about preserving the character and the heritage aspects of the buildings. These days a converted barn must look like a barn on the outside, and planners raise particular problems about the number and size of the new windows that can be inserted into the walls. This can be a serious drawback because barns were never built with windows and are naturally dark buildings.

In structural terms there are limitations to what can be achieved. There can be restricted headroom on the upper floor because of the roof trusses, which means that many barns have only two or three bedrooms, even though the overall square footage leaves scope for several more. Planners also limit the development of the garden, often insisting that most of the surrounding acreage is left as paddocks rather than landscaped into garden, and they can refuse permission for adjacent garages.

None of this has dampened the popularity of barns, but the supply has dried up. This means that prices have risen steeply, and it is questionable whether you can buy these buildings sufficiently cheaply to be able to convert them at a profit. You can expect to pay between £200,000 and £400,000 for a decent individual unconverted barn in the southern counties of England, and you should budget for spending the same amount of money again on the conversion work.

Completed conversions done to a high standard command a premium over other residential property. There are smaller conversions available within converted complexes, and these are significantly cheaper to buy if you want the lifestyle but have only limited funds available.

Outbuildings

With the trend for working from home gathering pace, purchasers of country houses are looking for properties with outbuildings. Disused stables or storage blocks are ripe for conversion to offices or granny annexes. Some buyers see the outbuildings as a money-making opportunity, producing accommodation to let as office space or, if they are in the right location, as holiday cottages. The use to which these outbuildings can be put will depend on the local authority's planning policy.

The costs of conversion will match the price of any other building work, so before you begin make sure that your returns will be adequate to match the cost of the renovations and that it will not result in making the overall property less attractive to buyers.

Pubs

As barn conversions have sprung up across the Home Counties, in towns the fashion has been to buy up old pubs and convert them to residential use. Large brewing companies have been selling off many of their old tied pubs in the inner cities as people have shown a preference for drinking in wine bars and restaurants. The buildings appeal to potential buyers because they are located in residential areas and are cheaper per square foot than buying a conventional house.

Pubs built in the 1920s and 1930s were often large, with two floors of extensive living space above the ground-floor pub, and many developers have turned the buildings into flats. The biggest design challenge in converting a pub lies in the treatment of the ground floor, which often has large windows set close to the pavement and therefore lacks privacy. Extensive use of opaque glass has helped. Internally, the decision has to be made whether to preserve the bar or any of the pub fittings. Imaginative kitchen design can go some way to overcoming these problems.

Pub conversions in rural areas are more problematic because planners regard the village pub as a local amenity and are usually unwilling to see a change of use. Many buyers have come unstuck over this and are often forced to preserve one room on the ground floor for business use.

Other buildings

Many other types of building come up for conversion, and if you get in before they become too fashionable they offer good value for money. Schools, chapels, railway stations, small banks, post offices, redundant offices and factories have all been snapped up. Inner-city fire stations and garage forecourts are likely to become increasingly available over the next few years. You may find yourself in competition with developers for these sites. They can create a larger number of smaller units and are, therefore, prepared to pay more for the land than anyone looking to find a house. Do your sums carefully and take advice from local agents. You will need plenty of patience and imagination, but you will have the satisfaction of building an unusual home.

Summary: Creating Space

- Buyers will pay a premium if the layout of the internal space exactly meets their needs and feels right.
- Badly laid out properties can be bought cheaply; reorganizing space is one of the best ways of making a profit.
- Private and public zones should be clearly defined and separated, but some flexibility allows buyers to adapt to their own needs.
- Avoid piecemeal alterations to preserve a sense of integrity and wholeness.
- The best solution is one that solves most of the problems.
- Making better use of existing space is the cheapest option, often involving no structural work.
- It is cheaper to extend upwards and downwards than sideways because the foundations already exist.
- If adding new space, ensure the property remains balanced.

Planning considerations

Analyse the existing space in terms of: headroom, daylight and air, circulation (of people), zoning, utilities, weatherproofing and exterior changes. Offset the cost against the increased value of the property or potential for profit.

Key considerations for specific renovations are:

- **Loft conversions:** headroom, windows and light, access, insulation, structural strength and permissions.
- **Basement conversions:** separation of access and utilities, headroom, windows and light, quality of access stairs, damp, and floors.
- **Back extensions:** dealing with the 'dogleg'.
- **Garage and porch conversions:** relatively easy but unlikely to add much value.
- **Conservatories:** position, style and permissions; often add little value.
- **Whole building conversions:** barns (now in short supply, expensive and subject to planning restrictions), outbuildings (ensure your returns will be adequate and that the overall property will still be attractive to buyers) and pubs (check you can get permission for change of use).

9 Making Improvements

The jobs described in this chapter cover the boring work on the fabric of your house that must be done if you really want to add value. They are dirty, expensive and disruptive, but they are the way you can make a profit because most people do not want to be bothered with them and will therefore pay a premium for a property where someone else has done them already.

Subsidence

This is the one word in a surveyor's report that causes most buyers to pull out. If you want to make money out of renovating properties, sorting out a house with subsidence is brave but financially rewarding. It usually requires underpinning or, where there is movement on the walls, partial demolition and rebuilding. You can sometimes get away with wall ties, which act as a brace to tie the structure together.

It is easy to detect if a house has suffered any movement. Check that the windows are level and whether there are any cracks in the brickwork. Stand underneath the front or back door and look up to check that the wall is vertical. If there is a bulge, there has been some movement.

Many houses built in and before the 19th century do not have foundations. They rest on clay, and in a hot summer the clay contracts, and cracks in the wall appear. The virtue of these houses is that the bricks originally used were much softer than those used today, and the walls tend to be thicker, so the property can tolerate some movement. If the movement is old, it may not be necessary to undertake repairs.

Another cause of subsidence is bomb damage incurred during the Blitz of the Second World War. Even though this happened a long time ago, many London terraces suffered from settlement and needed partial rebuilding. In an unmodernized house, it will not necessarily have been done. A more recent cause of subsidence is damage from the roots of trees. Weeping willows and other relatives of the willow are particularly dangerous, but any tree that has been planted too close to a house will cause problems before long.

Mortgage finance has become difficult to obtain on properties with subsidence and movement, so if you have a property that shows signs of subsidence, this is one job you cannot overlook. Consult a structural engineer about the work that is required, and if you are in any doubt, you should ask the local district surveyor for his opinion. You will, in any case, need the approval of the local district surveyor that the work has been done to a satisfactory standard.

If you live in an area that is prone to subsidence you may find you have trouble getting insurance, even when you have done the necessary underpinning, and that the premiums are expensive. Check what your costs might be before proceeding.

Drains

Drains carry away dirty water and soil from a property. They are usually located under manholes. If you have a problem with the drains, you won't remain ignorant of it for long, and a smell of bad eggs will pervade the house. Often, drains are blocked simply by an accumulation of grease, coffee grounds and

Above Subsidence is caused by the soil shrinking underneath the foundations of a building. This is a particular problem in areas with clay soils, or where a tree has been planted too close to a house. The obvious sign is a crack in the wall, running from a window or doorway and following the line of the mortar between the bricks. A house with severe subsidence will need underpinning and tying. A structural surveyor will be able to tell you whether the tree needs to be removed, and the local authority will say whether this is permitted in your area.

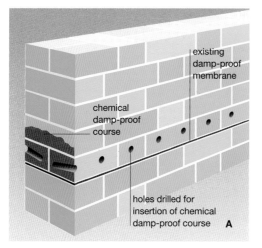

existing
damp-proof
membrane

chemical
damp-proof
course

holes drilled for
insertion of chemical
damp-proof course **A**

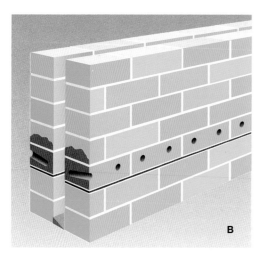

B

Above To remedy
a failed damp-proof
membrane in a (A)
solid or (B) cavity wall,
a chemical damp-proofer
is inserted into the wall,
both inside and outside.
This is messy and should
be undertaken before
any decoration is done.

other detritus that should not have been put
down the sink, and a plumber with a set of rods
will quickly clear this out. Sometimes baths and
showers can smell where the trap, which lies
below the plughole, is too small for the quantity
of water it takes.

More serious problems arise if a drain has
cracked. Modern technology enables specialists
to use cameras to explore drains without having
to dig up your basement first, but if the news is
bad you will have a large building project on
your hands because the pipes lie some way
beneath the floor, which has to be dug out.

Damp-proofing

If there is a problem with damp in a property
you can usually smell it. The air will be slightly
musty. Other signs are flaking paint, patches
of mould, salts coming through the plaster or
crumbling plasterwork. Vendors may use tricks
to disguise the problem – beware if the central
heating is on in summer, for instance – but they
are wasting their time because a surveyor will
use a special meter to register moisture in walls
and will quickly uncover a damp problem.

You should treat the surveyor's report on
damp with a degree of caution, however. The
meter registers moisture on and just inside the
wall's surface, but this does not automatically
mean that the property is suffering from rising
damp. There may simply be insufficient
ventilation or condensation from a bathroom
that needs an extractor fan.

If you want to check if there is moisture
in the brickwork, you should call in a specialist
damp firm and get them to drill into the brick to
establish how far the wet penetrates. If it is right

through the wall there is a problem, but you should check the cause before assuming that you have to buy their recommended chemical damp-proofing. It may be a problem outside the house, such as poor guttering or a patio that is set at too high a level, or an adjoining wall with no damp-proof course.

Houses built since the 1930s usually have a physical damp-proof course inserted between the bricks 15–30cm (6–12in) above the ground. This is usually a membrane of bitumized felt or plastic, which prevents damp rising from the ground up the walls. Houses built before these materials became available can be treated with a chemical damp-proof course, which is injected into the walls and covered inside with hydroscopic plaster. Some types of older property are not suitable for a chemical damp-proof course – if the wall is not constructed of brick, for instance. Usually, these properties are listed, and English Heritage will be able to advise on suitable ways for managing damp that concur with their regulations.

Chemical damp-proof courses do not last for ever and need redoing, usually after 10–20 years. Although many damp-proof firms offer lengthy guarantees, in practice they are hard to enforce, because the companies adduce numerous reasons the treatment has failed as a result of negligence on the owner's part in breach of the agreement.

Some properties or areas of a property are prone to damp, notably basements. If they have been excavated out below pavement level, a chemical damp-proof course will have to be injected. Similarly houses built on a hill, often with a retaining wall into a hill, will need tanking.

Walls and brickwork

Most British houses are made of brick or, at least, faced in brick even if steel frames and breezeblocks have been used inside. As long as the cement pointing is in good condition and the bricks have not been rendered, there is little reason a brick wall should decay; it can stand for several hundred years.

This longevity is just as well, because the dearth of specialist workmen is particularly acute among bricklayers. Developers building new houses are increasingly relying on steel frames and prefabrication in factories in an attempt to overcome the skill shortage, but for the average home owner who is faced with the need to repair a wall, the labour shortage will become increasingly problematic.

It is sometimes necessary to repoint brickwork when the mortar has worn away to the point that there is a risk that water will penetrate the bricks. Mortar should always be softer than the bricks so that it takes the stress of movement and frost damage. Unfortunately, in old houses bricks are often softer than the hard cement mortars that are now used for repointing. Water can get trapped behind the cement mortar, and this damages the surface of the bricks. You should insist that the builder uses a lime and sand mortar if you have old bricks. It may take more time and money, but it is worth the additional investment.

Waterproof external coatings or renderings, such as pebbledash and stone cladding, are liable to crack from frost, which allows water to penetrate behind them, leading to damp problems. Brick walls should not be rendered, and it is best to remove any old rendering.

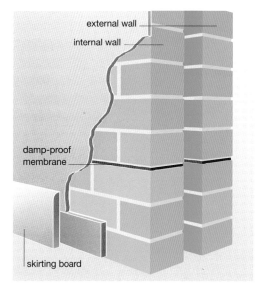

external wall

internal wall

damp-proof membrane

skirting board

Above Most modern buildings in Britain have cavity walls, consisting of two layers of bricks, or breeze-blocks inside and brick outside, with a gap between them, which helps stop damp getting in. The damp-proof membrane should be at least two bricks above ground level. The interior wall is usually plastered, or plasterboarded, and finished off with a skirting board.

Cavity wall construction began in the 1870s and became widespread over the next hundred years. It was believed that cavity walls were more stable and provided better insulation against heat loss and protection from wind and rain than the old solid walls. While there is nothing wrong with this in theory, cavity walls were often not well built. The risk with a cavity wall is water penetration, which will show up as damp patches on the wall. The remedy is to remove some of the external bricks and clear out the obstruction. External coatings to the brick wall will not solve the problem. If the inner wall is made up of a timber frame, any rain penetration will cause the wood to rot, so this is not a problem that should be left untreated.

If the wall shows signs of cracks, you should consult a surveyor or structural engineer. A hairline crack may have a number of causes, some of which could be serious. In particular, you want to guard against cracking from movement (see subsidence, page 96). Newer houses, which are built of harder bricks and cement mortars, are more susceptible to cracking than old houses, which can tolerate more movement.

Windows

Replacing rotten or ugly windows can add considerably to the value of your property because they transform the external appearance. Windows have frames that can be made of wood, metal or uPVC. You need to select windows that are in keeping with the age of the house. Sash windows, for example, were always made of wooden box frames and should always be replaced with windows in the same style. Metal window frames suffer from condensation and are susceptible to rust unless regularly painted. Nonetheless, in some types of loft conversion or in an Art Deco property you should not replace them.

The uPVC window has become ubiquitous in modern houses as manufacturers assure buyers that they will last a lifetime. They promise no maintenance because the frames will not rot or rust. Unfortunately, plastic is not exempt from the laws of decay. Over time it becomes brittle and discolours. Eventually, the sealed double-glazed units will mist up; how quickly this happens will depend on the quality of materials used and the workmanship.

If you have timber windows that have been neglected and left unpainted for a number of years, it may be possible to repair them without going to the expense of replacing them. A carpenter can chisel out the old putty, cut in new sections of timber to replace any rotten wood and reseal with fresh putty. It is a labour-intensive task, but it is preferable to replacing the windows.

New regulations, which came into force in April 2002, stipulate that all windows in new homes and replacement windows have to conform to thermal insulation standards set out in the Building Regulations. In effect, this means that windows now have to be double glazed in sealed units with low emissivity glass. This does not mean that you have to replace timber frames with uPVC, but the new frames will be slightly thicker than the old ones, and you will need a skilful carpenter to install them.

Replacement windows

Double glazing is a popular home improvement for many home owners. In addition to saving heat and cutting draughts, it also cuts down noise, which is especially important if you live on a busy road or near an airport. You need to ensure that double-glazed units are manufactured to BSI standard BS5713, and you should shop around to get an idea of differing qualities. Some companies will provide a 10-year guarantee, but it can often be hard to ensure that these are genuine. Source your supplier from one of the official double-glazing trade associations.

Double glazing adds little value to a property. It will take many years to recover the costs in reduced heating bills, and unless you are on a busy road, buyers consider it a pleasing extra rather than an essential. So take care before the salesman's patter seduces you. If you value it though, you should go ahead because it will not detract from the value of the property.

You need to check whether you need planning permission or building regulation approval for replacement windows. This is likely to apply if you live in a listed building or a local conservation area. The average cost of replacing all windows in a three-bedroom, semi-detached house in uPVC is around £6,000. On top of that you will have to add a sum for replastering and redecoration after the work has been done.

If you do not have permission to replace the windows, or do not want to alter the appearance of your house, you can install secondary double glazing. Essentially a glazed frame fitted to the inside of a window frame, secondary double glazing offers the same benefits as ordinary double glazing in terms of noise and heat-loss reduction.

Joists

The joists are the timbers that run between the walls of a house and support the floors and ceilings. If you buy a property that has been neglected for decades you may have to replace the joists. This is expensive, both because of the cost of the materials and because of the labour involved. If you think you might have to do this, factor a generous allowance for the work into your budget.

Roofs

Most roofs in English houses are pitched, with the tiles or slates and felting resting on cut timbers known as the rafters. This is probably the best design for houses in this country, because it allows the heavy annual rainfall to run away naturally. Flat roofs, on the other hand, have a tendency to collect water.

Houses built in the 19th century or earlier sometimes have valley roofs, which slope down to a central gully. Valley roofs need more maintenance because the gully gets blocked with leaves and debris washing down, and they have to be cleared every couple of years. Over time, the gully can become porous, letting water penetrate through to the ceiling below. You can line it with bitumen, which can seal it for a few years, but eventually the gully may have to be replaced altogether.

Pitched roofs have a life of about 70 years, but they do need maintenance. In particular, you should take early action if you see slates that are slipping or gutters that are blocked or perished around the joints. Flashings that cover the edges also wear out and need replacing every so often. Slate roofs do eventually fail

when the nails holding them in place rust through. If you are suffering continually from slates falling off, it may be time to consider having the roof stripped and recovered. You can reuse some of the slates to save money.

If the property you are purchasing has been so neglected that there is no other option than a new roof, you should expect to spend anything upwards of £4,000 – the cost will, of course, depend on the size of the house. Slates are more expensive than tiles, but you should not put tiles on a roof built originally for slates, because they will be too heavy for the timbers, causing them to sink and setting up problems with leaks.

A cheaper option is to cover the tiles in bitumen, but this is unlikely to last and means that the tiles cannot be reused. It will actually detract from the value of the property on resale because it signals to a purchaser that the roof has been cheaply repaired and is likely to need renewing. Surveyors are quick to recommend that the roof needs redoing within a year or two if there is any doubt about its condition, so it is worth doing any work properly. A recovered roof can last for another 60 years.

Flat roofs

Flat roofs are commonly found on extensions and are notoriously prone to leaking. The covering, which is usually asphalt, rests on timbers that have to be sturdily constructed so that they don't sag over time. The roof has to be set at a slight gradient (no less than 1:60) in order to allow adequate drainage. Water tends to pond or collect in puddles in dips on the surface. This eventually finds tiny holes and starts to leak through. You must maintain the asphalt regularly, because it is easily damaged by heavy snow, hail or rain. Flat roofs tend to last for 15–20 years before they need to be replaced.

Gutters

Careful maintenance of the gutters is essential to stop other problems arising. A broken gutter will mean that water will pour down the walls rather than soak away into a drain. The water will eventually penetrate the brick, causing damp problems and, possibly, rot among the timbers.

Most modern gutters are made of plastic, but in time this tends to crack and split as it contracts and expands with temperature. Old-fashioned cast-iron guttering is much more efficient, but it is difficult to find workmen with the skills to maintain it, and their charges are usually high. Nevertheless, if you have cast-iron gutters, try to repair rather than replace them wherever possible.

Central heating

A good heating system is an essential component in a modernized property. As most houses now have some form of heating, many buyers see it as a necessity; a recent survey by a building society showed it to be the third most important factor on buyers' lists. You will always get your money back when you spend on heating. An old system is likely to reduce the value of the house by a similar amount.

Just as important as having a heating system in the first place is keeping it up to date. Boilers have a life of about 10 years. They can last longer, but they become increasingly inefficient as they age, leading to a consequent

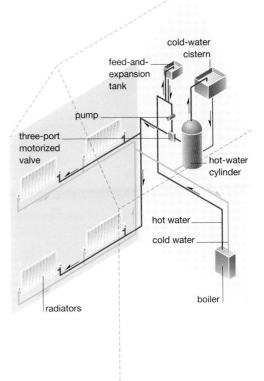

cold-water cistern

feed-and-expansion tank

pump

three-port motorized valve

hot-water cylinder

hot water

cold water

boiler

radiators

Above In a modern central-heating system, hot water from the boiler is pumped into the hot-water cylinder and from there to the radiators as needed. The feed-and-expansion tank ensures that the system neither overflows nor runs dry. Large-bore systems are inefficient and cost more to run, so it may be cost-effective to install a new system.

rise in heating bills. A new boiler will be considerably more energy efficient than the one you are likely to be replacing. You can, for example, expect to reduce the annual gas bill by about one-third in the average house just by replacing the boiler.

There is no such thing as a standard central-heating system – you have to design one to suit your needs. Begin by looking for one that uses the cheapest fuel, and in today's market this probably means mains gas, although this is not an option for everyone. You don't have to live too far out of a town before you lose access to a gas main. For many people in the country an oil-fired system is the only realistic alternative, and this means being faced with a hefty bill when the oil tanker delivers.

Other fuel options are bottled gas (LPG) and solid fuel. Solid fuel, such as wood and coal, is not an option in London and other large conurbations, which are smokeless zones. Coal is also dirty. LPG is expensive, costing about three times as much as gas. Each has its pros and cons, and you should consult a central-heating engineer for advice on your property and locality.

If you intend to rent out your property, you should consider a modern electric boiler, because the Landlord and Tenant Act requires that a gas-fired system in a rented property must be regularly inspected and plumbers' charges for this service have risen steeply in the last few years. Electricity is about twice as expensive as gas, but the tenants will pay their own heating bills. Night-storage heaters, which run on a cheaper electricity tariff than is available in during the day, are a popular option, but they

do not heat the house effectively in the evening, just when you need the heating on, and you will need an additional heat source, such as a fire, to be really warm and comfortable.

Choosing a boiler

The government has stipulated that new and replacement boilers must be energy-efficient. A condensing boiler can reduce your bills by up to 35 per cent, but it may not be suitable for your property. Beyond that, the choice is between boilers that run off a cold-water storage system or run straight from the mains.

A combination boiler heats both water and heating water straight from the mains as you use it. This means that you can remove the water tank and the hot-water cylinder, which is a convenient way of saving space. The boiler is more expensive than a traditional system and needs more maintenance. Combination boilers are best used in flats, where the amount of hot water used is limited, and they cannot service more than one bathroom at the same time. They become less efficient when water has to be pumped some distance or up several floors. Showers are not that effective with a combination boiler, because there isn't sufficient pressure, and you might find a separate electric shower a better option. The boilers must be placed against an external wall with 60cm (about 24in) between it and an open window.

Cold-water storage systems are the traditional central-heating system where a cold-water tank, usually in the loft, is fed from the mains water, and the tank then feeds the boiler and the hot-water cylinder. When you draw hot water from the tap, it comes from the hot-water cylinder, which is replenished from the cold-water tank. This system has the advantage that the supply of hot water can be plentiful (provided the cylinder has the capacity) and is most suitable for family houses.

Plumbers are increasingly installing megaflow systems in family houses. These systems run directly off the mains but over come the disadvantages of combination boilers. For example, because the water is at mains pressure already, the system requires no pump to achieve power shower performance. They are more expensive than a conventional system.

A critical decision is the size of your boiler in terms of heat capacity or Btu. You should consult a central-heating engineer rather than a plumber for advice if you are unsure. Central heating is a complex area and not all plumbers know enough about new technology. If the boiler is too small it will be unable to heat all the radiators adequately. If it is too large you will waste money. A central-heating engineer will also advise you on the number and size of the radiators you need for each room.

Radiators

In the last decade radiators have become much more exciting. Instead of the boring, flat, wall panel you can choose from cast-iron reproductions and exciting modern styles, ranging from ladder designs to a metal copy of a plant. These are much more expensive than an ordinary radiator, but they can look attractive in rooms such as bathrooms or halls. They do not in themselves add value but will contribute to the overall appearance of a stylish property, which may be reflected in the total value.

Inefficient radiators

If your central-heating system is inefficient, even if the boiler is new, you should investigate whether too much air is getting into the system. Over a number of years this leads to a build-up of sludge in the pipes and radiators, and eventually this will cause the radiators to rust and spring leaks. One option could be to seal the system and power-flush the radiators to remove the sludge. The cost will depend on the size of your system.

Cost and timing

The installation of a central-heating system is a job for the professionals. You can change radiators yourself, but unless you have the requisite CORGI qualifications, it is illegal even to buy a boiler, let alone install one.

Installing a central-heating system will probably take about two weeks, and you should bear in mind that the floorboards have to come up so that the copper pipes can be laid. Your kitchen or utility room may also have to be rearranged to accommodate a new boiler, and space will have to be made for a hot-water tank if you have decided against a combination boiler.

For the average three-bedroom house you can expect to pay £3,000–£4,000 for a new central-heating system. If you want to change the boiler it will probably cost you £1,000–£1,500, of which the bulk will be the cost of the labour involved.

Right Houses built only a few years ago may not have enough sockets for all of the electrical appliances needed in a modern home. If the ring main is in good condition it is possible to run spurs from it to provide extra sockets where needed. It is a relatively simple task for an electrician and is probably worth undertaking, before decorating starts, as not having enough sockets may be a deal-breaker.

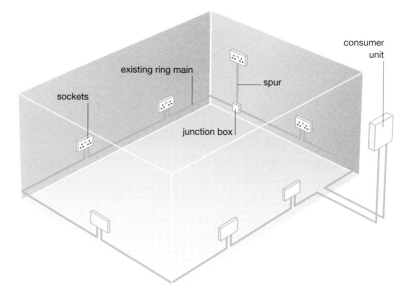

consumer unit

existing ring main

spur

sockets

junction box

Wiring

The electrical wiring in a house should be renewed every 25–30 years, because the wires become brittle over time and there is an increased risk of fire. In addition, what used to be known as the fuse box and is now called the consumer board should also be changed if it is more than 20 years old. Modern consumer boards have trip switches rather than old-fashioned fuse wire and are much safer.

Houses that were wired before the Second World War have systems based on 15-amp circuits, and the plugs lack fuses. If your house has this system, the plugs will have round pins. Any house with such a system needs rewiring completely, because not only is it unsuitable for modern appliances, but it is now so old as to be dangerous. Do not try to get away with just adding 13-amp sockets, which will run the risk of overloading the wire and causing a fire. Houses wired from the 1950s onwards are based on ring-main systems, in which all the wires run to a fuse box and the sockets are 13-amp. There are different circuits for different parts of the house and for large appliances, such as a cooker, which consumes a lot of power. It is easy to install additional circuits to increase capacity.

You can expect to spend about £3,000 on rewiring an entire house, although this will depend on the size of the house and number of sockets you install. The bulk of the cost will be labour, because the materials themselves are not that expensive.

If you have to undertake rewiring take the opportunity to install state-of-the-art technology. It is now possible to wire your house to a central computer that controls all applications, including the CD player, television, video and DVD. Speakers can be built into the ceilings in bathrooms, bedrooms and kitchens, and adjusted according to individual taste. The heating and lighting can be controlled from the same point. At present this is expensive, but these systems will get cheaper and are likely to be standard in expensive properties in the next 10–15 years.

Staircases

Most people pay little attention to the staircases in their houses. In standard houses from the 19th and 20th centuries often the only thought given to the stairs is the decision on the colour of the paint for the balustrades and the type of floor covering. This is a pity because it is an important element in terms of both design and function. Just consider that the staircase is usually the dominant feature of a hallway and it is the first thing that any visitors see when they enter a house.

In functional terms stairs are the pivotal link between floors, and in modern, architect-designed houses this fact is sometimes recognized by the emphasis that is given to its sculptural form. In many lofts in urban centres, the staircase has become a dominant design feature, and it may even be made of non-traditional materials, such as glass or concrete, to emphasize the modernity of the conversion and the escape it offers from traditional suburban constraints.

Above A stylish way to maximize space is to insert a spiral staircase, which hardly interrupts the flow of light and can be an attractive feature in itself.

Stairways come in many forms. They can be open within a room, enclosed by walls, attached to a wall or be free-standing; they may even serve as a room divider. The most important considerations, however, are safety, especially for families with young children, and ease of movement up and down. A staircase must support the comings and goings of people and from time to time of furniture. It must be supported in turn by walls, posts or beams that transfer the load it carries to the foundations.

The staircase is composed of risers and treads, and the width and depth of these make the staircase either steep or easy to climb. All risers in a run of stairs should be the same height and all treads be of the same depth, otherwise there is a risk that people will trip. Headroom is another important factor. You need a clearance of at least 2m (6ft 6in) between the stairs and the ceiling on a landing.

Many traditional houses are dominated by a narrow, straight-up staircase, but other stair plans can be used even within a narrow hall. The arrangement you adopt will depend on the direction of access to the stairs at both levels and the space available. A staircase takes up a lot of space, and you do not want to sacrifice valuable living space in the adjacent rooms. A variation on the straight staircase in a traditional house is the L-shape. Here the run of stairs is broken by a landing halfway. The stairs then turn through 90 degrees. The size of the halfway landing should be as deep as the stairs are wide.

Other possible arrangements are U-shaped staircases, which turn through 180 degrees and are best sited at the end of a hall, and spiral staircases, which are useful where space is at a premium. Bear in mind that more stringent fire regulations have limited the use of spiral staircases into lofts, for instance, so check with the local authority that your intended staircase is permitted under their rules.

During the 1960s and 1970s stairs with open risers were fashionable. These stairs, in which the stair treads have no backs, are light and airy and are useful if the staircase has to be placed against a window, for instance, or if you want to minimize the visual separation between the two floors. However, if you are restoring an older house that was 'modernized' in the 1960s you would be well advised to remove such a staircase, which is out of character in this type of house, and replace it with a more traditional structure that is in keeping.

Under the stairs

Space under the stairs is often neglected but can be used for additional storage. Put cupboard doors on any space you create, or you may end up with a hallway that looks cluttered and untidy.

Handrails and balustrades

For reasons of safety a handrail is required on any open side of a staircase. The rails can be objects of great elegance and beauty with wonderful curves, particularly in Georgian houses, and the balustrades or railings supporting the handrail can be carved into luscious shapes or left plain.

The choice of balustrade can make a significant contribution to the overall feel of the property. Open, scarcely visible balustrades made of thin wire, which run horizontally rather like railings on a yacht, have moved from the office into the home, where they can create a feeling of space and openness. Glass balustrades will complement glass staircases and keep a sense of light flowing through the building. Heavy, ornate staircases are out of fashion at present, but there is no doubt that they can create a sense of grandeur in even a modest house, provided the hall is wide enough to take such an ornate feature.

Summary: Making Improvements

People will pay a premium for not having to do dirty, expensive, disruptive work to the fabric of the house.

- **Subsidence:** mortgages and insurance can be difficult to get on properties with subsidence and movement. Sorting it is brave but financially rewarding. Consult a structural engineer and the district surveyor.
- **Drains:** major problems involve a large building project as pipes lie beneath the floor which has to be dug out.
- **Damp-proofing:** signs of damp are a musty smell, flaking paint, patches of mould, salts coming through plaster or crumbling plasterwork. Try to establish the cause and how far the damp penetrates.
- **Walls and brickwork:** if a wall has cracks, consult a structural engineer or surveyor. Problems may arise with cement pointing, cavity walls and external coatings. Skilled bricklayers are scarce.

- **Windows:** replacing rotten or ugly windows adds considerable value – you may need planning permission or building regulation approval.
- **Joists:** replacing joists in a neglected house is expensive and labour-intensive.
- **Roofs:** maintain gutters rigorously to prevent many problems. Do the job properly if you do need to replace the roof, avoiding cheaper quick-fixes.
- **Central heating:** good heating is regarded as a necessity. You will always get your money back. Consult a central-heating engineer rather than a plumber. Work must be carried out by registered professionals.
- **Wiring:** should be renewed every 25–30 years. Central computers controlling all applications are likely to become standard over the next 10–15 years.
- **Staircases:** safety and ease of movement are essential, but consider alternative plans and materials to improve value.

Part 3
The House
in Detail

10 First Impressions

In the type of survey beloved by estate agents, you will find reports about how the majority of buyers make up their mind to buy a house in the first 40 seconds before they have even crossed the threshold. This suggests either that buyers are impulsive and irrational or that location is the most significant factor in their decision. The latter is the more plausible explanation, so before you begin work on the inside of your property, take a long, hard look at the outside.

The façade

The initial impressions of the house formed while the buyer is waiting for you to answer the front door, or for the estate agent to work out how the locks undo, are nonetheless important in creating an idea about whether this is a well-maintained house or one that has been left to run down. It can determine how close any offers to buy are to your asking price. So some cosmetic attention to the frontage of your property will pay off.

Boundaries

One project well worth the investment is to replace old railings in front of a period house if they have been lost over the decades. Many of these railings were ripped out in the Second World War and replaced by ugly low walls of brick or, even worse, painted breezeblocks. You can expect to pay around £1,200 to reinstate railings in front of a Victorian property about 5m (16ft) wide, and you will create an immediate impression of quality.

If you live in a property that was built after railings were no longer used as the front boundary, you have a choice between brick walls, fencing or a simple hedge. A brick wall is the best option. If you choose fencing it will probably look better in a town if it is fairly plain and painted white or dark green. A well-maintained hedge of yew or beech is attractive and evergreen, but it takes time to grow and needs regular clipping.

Windows and skylights

No matter what type of property you have, there is only one rule: the style of the window should match the period of the house. This means that uPVC windows should be avoided unless the

Above Georgian town houses are traditionally fenced with iron railings in order to allow as much light as possible to fall into the working quarters in the basement. Make sure that they fit in with the style of your property and, if necessary, replace broken ones and repaint them.

Above Brick walls suit many types of property, from cottages to Victorian terraces and modern homes. When doing repairs to the front of the house, don't forget to get the wall repointed or the gate rehung and painted. First impressions count.

house was built in the last 20 years. In houses that were built before the 1930s the windows should always have wooden frames, while some houses that were built between the 1930s and 1980s had windows with aluminium or metal frames, which should, if possible, be replaced.

Dressing the windows

Choosing the appropriate dressing for the windows is important when it comes to showing off your house to the best advantage. Curtains or blinds control the light, obscure an undesirable view, conceal us from the neighbours and provide insulation from the cold and protection from the heat. They are not just about decoration, therefore, and you must give careful thought to your choice. Above all, however, a window is an architectural feature, and if the windows in your property are distinctive, they should be dressed in a way that does not detract from this.

Until fairly recently most people chose fairly plain window dressings, with the emphasis on uncluttered blinds and unpatterned curtains. This style is now giving way to a more decorative style, but no matter what the fashion, you should furnish the window in accordance with the room's function and the degree of natural light.

Skylights

Skylights can brighten an indoor space even on grey winter days. They are essential additions to windowless rooms if there is scope to install them, and in rooms where there are already windows, they can enhance a dark corner or balance the light if too much comes from one source – in a long, narrow room lit by windows at only one end, for example.

When you are deciding where to position a skylight, you should take into account a number of factors. The closer a skylight is to an interior wall surface, the more light will be reflected, and this is the way to gain maximum benefit. If you paint the walls white, you will add to this effect because white serves as a reflector.

Skylights are usually manufactured in standard sizes, so your choice will be determined to some extent by the room you are illuminating. In a loft conversion, for instance, the lower the pitch of the roof, the longer the window needs to be to get the best possible views. You can put several windows side by side or one above another to create

---

The front of your house

Here are some simple rules to guarantee that the front of your house makes a good impression on potential buyers:

- Make sure that the house is easy to find, with the number or name clearly visible.
- Hide the dustbins and clear up all litter and debris around the front entrance.
- Put some windowboxes or planters in the front area if there is one and fill them with seasonal bedding, but remember to keep the plants watered because there is nothing more depressing than dead foliage.
- Cut back and clear away all overgrown plants in the front garden.
- Paint the front door – don't use anything except dark blue, black, dark green or bright red – and clean the door furniture.
- Install adequate security: a front door must have a five-lever lock for insurance purposes.
- Repaint flaking stucco every few years, rubbing it down with a wire brush before to remove the surface dirt.
- Repair and repaint windows where necessary.

---

an attractive effect. Try to get the glazed area up to the equivalent of 20 per cent of the floor area and use several smaller windows rather than one or two large ones.

It is essential to keep skylights weathertight. Because they are placed in the roof they are more exposed to the elements than windows in a wall. Their surface must shed water efficiently, and the perimeter must be protected by flashing where it abuts the roof. Skylight manufacturers supply several different flashings, so choose one that is compatible with your existing roofing material.

Skylights must also be glazed with special glass to minimize heat loss, provide adequate insulation and reduce the risk of accidents if workmen have to get on to the roof. You should also consider installing special blinds or operable shutters on the interior to protect against heat loss or too bright sunlight.

Internal doors

The style, grandeur and proportion of doors hint at the social aspirations of the owners of the house. If they are too ornate or overdone they can make the house unattractive, but if they are too plain they will make the house appear depressing and mean.

Doors look best if they match the period and style of architecture of the house. In a Victorian house, for example, replacing the flush doors that were often fitted in the 1960s with panelled doors is one of the simplest ways to bring a feeling of quality back into the property. You can add an impression of grandeur to a room by installing double doors, which give the feeling that this is a room into which one makes an entrance – but remember that the room must be of sufficient size and scale to take such a treatment.

If you live in a modern house with plain, flat doors you can add interest by changing the door handles. There is now a huge choice of designs, and an expensive handle will instantly lift a dull door.

If in keeping with the style of the house, glazed doors are a boon in houses that have dark corridors or hallways because they allow light to flow through the house. They are also attractive in lofts and converted warehouses where they can be taken up to the height of the ceiling, which adds a sense of drama to the room.

It has long been popular in older properties to strip wooden doors of their paint and leave the natural wood exposed. The quickest way to do this is to take the doors to be dipped in a tank of acid (usually caustic soda or something similar). The disadvantage of this is that it warps the doors and dissolves the glue holding the architrave and mountings to the door. If you can bear to spend the time, you should strip the doors with a gentler paint stripper and then sand them carefully, before applying a coat of matt varnish. You should then avoid having to use wood filler to glue the doors back together again. Bear in mind that the doors in Victorian houses were always intended to be painted, and so were made of cheap pine, which might look worse stripped.

Hanging doors

There are some practical considerations to take into account when you are hanging doors. For reasons of safety, a door should always open inwards into a room and never outwards into a hall or passageway. In bedrooms and bathrooms the door should be hung to ensure maximum privacy – so that the bed or the toilet are not immediately visible, for example – although in a small bathroom turning around the door opening can make the room look bigger and more spacious.

Living with the 1960s

Modern architecture may be fashionable again, but some decades produced buildings that remain forever unloved, particularly the boxy houses built during the 1960s. Concrete brutalism was the watchword of architects then, but the style never really found favour with the public, and houses built in this era are usually significantly cheaper than the perennially popular Victorian and Edwardian terraced properties farther down the street.

Improving a 1960s house

Rocketing house prices have persuaded some buyers to look again at 1960s houses. They can offer good value for money in excellent locations, and they often have more space inside than is found in more recently built properties. Some buyers are discovering that if they don't like the exterior, it can be changed, and if you are prepared to apply the principles of interior design to the outside of the house to transform its look and feel, you will undoubtedly increase the value.

When you are assessing the exterior begin with the windows. They are often out of proportion to the whole and are too large or too small. Picture windows were highly fashionable in the 1960s, but the bare expanse of glass can look intimidating now, especially if it forms part of an extension to an earlier house. Replacing metal-framed picture windows with wooden multi-pane windows will immediately create character and add value.

Porches should also be given careful consideration. Originally, these were often built to flank the front door but at a later date were filled in with glass to intergrate them with the rest of the house. Too small to become rooms in their own right, these areas are now used frequently for prams, bikes, roller skates and other hard-to-store items, creating an untidy impression as soon as you step through the front door. Knocking out the enclosure and reinstating the area as a porch will immediately render the exterior more elegant.

The next area to look at is the brickwork or other external rendering. If a house has been extended and the brickwork doesn't match the original, the house will look patchy and lack integrity. You can remedy this by adding handmade clay tiles or by painting the lower part of the wall. Alternatively, use timber cladding to create a New England effect. The same goes for the roof: you can replace a concrete tiled roof with slates and can change the gutters from plastic to powder-coated aluminium ones.

Security

Everyone wants a secure home, and when potential purchasers come to view your property one of the first things they will note is whether it is safe. Some properties tend to appear less secure than others – single women, for instance, rarely buy basement flats because they feel they might be more vulnerable to intruders – but these days all buyers will be assessing the level of protection against break-ins. People who have just moved house are frequent targets of burglars, and houses where builders are working are especially vulnerable, particularly as the burglar alarms might be switched off.

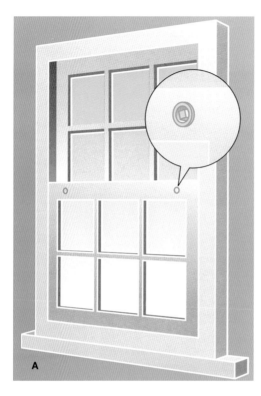

A

B

Above Sash windows (A) are very easy to break into. A simple way of preventing this is to fit dual-screw locks, in which a bolt is screwed through receivers that line up in the two sashes.

To secure casement windows (B) a variety of locks are available. The type shown here has a bolt on the window and a bolt case on the window frame. When the window is shut, the bolt locks automatically, but can only be opened with a key.

When you are determining how to secure your home, you need to get the balance right. You don't want to install too many locks and bolts, but a single Yale lock on the front door is inadequate these days, not least from the point of view of the insurance companies. The cost of your premiums can be reduced if you install security that complies with the companies' requirements, and on average you might expect a reduction in your premiums of 7.5 per cent if your alarm is professionally installed and maintained, of 12.5 per cent if the alarm automatically notifies the police and of 5 per cent if you have installed acceptable door and window locks.

The bare minimum is to have window locks on every window that opens at ground-floor and basement level and secure deadlocks on every door into the property. Beyond this you can start to exploit the benefits of modern technology. A video entry phone that enables you to see who is standing at the door when they call can protect you from all the doorstep salesmen who might have more sinister intentions. At the same time you need to install security lights so that you can see your unexpected callers after dark.

The next level is to install a burglar alarm. These represent serious deterrents for burglars, who will usually choose to break into a house down the street without an alarm. If you want to go down this route, you should call in a specialist firm to advise you on the best system for your house and locality. Systems vary enormously and you will need to think about how much you want the alarm to intrude into your personal life. Some alarms require certain doors in the house to be kept shut when the alarm is activated, and this could slow you down in leaving the house, so it may not be a good idea if your time is limited. Make sure when you install the system that the siren boxes are visible at both the front and back of the house so a burglar can clearly see that the house has an alarm. You can expect to spend between £1,000 and £2,000 on a burglar alarm system, and there will be a maintenance charge to the security company on top of this.

Other security measures are simple but effective. Install security lights outside the property that are activated by movement over the driveway. These are a good idea in country properties. In towns you could consider joining your local Neighbourhood Watch scheme. Timers that bring some lights in the property on early in the evening before you get home are also useful deterrents, especially when you are away on holiday.

Security in apartment blocks is often determined by the freeholder, but you will usually find that their appointed managing agent will listen readily to your requests, although you will have to pay for extra security in your service charges.

It is hard to quantify how much good security will add to the value of your property, if anything at all. It is more likely, however, that poor security will detract from the value because it gives an impression that the property is not well cared for. Apartment blocks are much more popular if they are securely maintained, and this will undoubtedly be reflected in the price you can get for your property.

Parking

Parking facilities are scarce in some city centres, and the value of an individual space, whether it is an off-street parking bay, an underground space or a garage, has soared way past the rise in general house prices in the last five years. People are less willing to leave their cars parked in a street because of the rising incidence of casual vandalism, and the simple shortage of residents' parking bays can leave people driving round and round the local streets when they come home late at night.

If you are buying a property and parking is an optional extra with the purchase, you should always include it. A parking space will remain a valuable and appreciating asset. The prices charged at new developments for parking spaces will give you an idea of how much value off-street parking can add to your property.

Building a garage

There is no faster way to knock money off the value of your property than to have an ugly garage tacked on to the side of the house. It is essential that the garage should be in keeping with the style of the property and, preferably, that it should be as unobtrusive as possible. Before you build a garage, you must check whether you need planning permission. In most areas you won't unless the garage is more than 20m (about 65ft) from the road boundary. There should be at least 5m (16ft) between the front of the garage and the boundary to allow space for a car in front.

Flat-roofed garages are particularly ugly and are likely to suffer from more water penetration than if you build one with a pitched roof, although this will be considerably more expensive. Ask your builder for quotes and advice and check that he is up to date with current building regulations.

Be prepared to spend money on good-quality doors, which will enhance the appearance of your property enormously and add value. Wood looks better than metal, but needs annual maintenance. Choose a solid hardwood, such as cedar, and paint it the same colour as the front door. Make sure you install a secure lock.

In inner-city suburbs many older properties have ugly single-storey garages alongside the house, built in the 1960s when planning permission was readily given. If you find that you use the garage for storage and not

for a car, consider knocking down the garage and using the space to add a side extension to the property. You may even be able to add an extra storey. Planning may be slow to come through, but the extension will add much more value to the house than a garage because you will be increasing the size of your property.

Common parts

This is the name given to the communal areas in a block of flats or converted house. The maintenance is usually the responsibility of the freeholder, and the leaseholders pay part of the service charge for the cleaning and upkeep. Sadly, many managing agents are remiss about their responsibilities, and in converted houses, where there are rarely managing agents, the common parts are a byword for looking shabby and neglected.

Some fairly simple steps are available to leaseholders to improve the appearance of these areas. The first is simply to keep the volume of junk mail and uncollected post under control. Every week throw out any junk mail that has accumulated. Do not allow other leaseholders to keep their bicycles, skis or other awkward-to-store equipment in the common parts: it is illegal for anything to be there that causes an obstruction to an escape route in the event of fire. Make sure that the dustbin area is concealed.

If the freeholder is not assiduous enough on the cleaning of the common parts you can choose to badger them until there is action or you can agree with your fellow leaseholders to establish a rota among yourselves. In particular, make sure that the windows are cleaned at least once or twice a year. You should also pay careful attention to the lighting. If the common parts are dark, install low-voltage halogen lighting and keep all the light bulbs functioning. This will go a long way towards brightening dead space.

A popular stratagem for livening up common parts is to place pot plants on the stairs. This usually backfires, however, as people forget to water and maintain them and they can end up making the area look more neglected.

Summary: First Impressions

- **Cosmetic attention to frontage** – façade, boundaries, windows and front door – will pay off as initial impressions are important. See page 115 for a checklist.
- **Windows:** the style should match the period of the house. Dressings are important, too. Skylights can brighten indoor spaces considerably.
- **Interior doors:** should match the period and architecture of the house. Glazed doors help brighten dark corridors and hallways. Expensive handles will instantly lift a dull door. Stripping wooden doors is popular, but the wood may not be up to it, and strong chemicals can damage the glue and warp the wood. Doors should always open inwards; hang them for maximum privacy in bedrooms and bathrooms.
- **Improving 1960s houses:** replace the windows, re-open boxed-in porches, paint or clad unsightly brickwork in wood, replace concrete roof tiles and ugly guttering.

- **Security:** good security may not add value, but poor security will detract from the value. The bare minimum is window locks on ground-floor windows and dead locks on all doors. Extras are video entry phones, security lights and a burglar alarm.
- **Parking:** always take a parking space if it is an optional extra – it will remain a valuable and appreciating asset, particularly in city centres. Garages should be unobtrusive and in keeping with the style of the property. Ugly garages seriously errode the value of a house. Consider replacing it with a side extension, especially where space demands are a premium.
- **Common parts:** encourage all leaseholders to clear junk mail, keep windows clean and lights functioning, conceal dustbins and remove awkward-to-store equipment.

11 The Kitchen

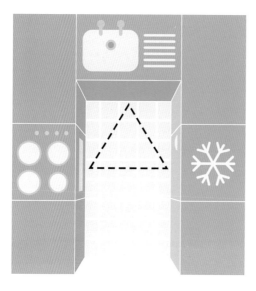

The kitchen is the most important room in the house when it comes to adding value to a property. Kitchens have moved a long way in the last 20 years from being purely functional rooms, and changes in equipment, materials and lifestyles mean that we now use kitchens differently. The emphasis is on creating an attractive living space as much as a utilitarian service room.

Adding value

The ability to exploit the potential of the kitchen space to promote this dual function of living space and practical working place will determine how much more your property can be worth after remodelling. Estate agents define this success as a kitchen that works both as a status symbol and a statement of lifestyle but that is still practicable and robust enough for the hard wear and tear of daily use. They are unanimous that a good kitchen will often clinch the deal for a buyer and that many other faults in a property can be overlooked if this room is right. The general advice is that you should spend about 5 per cent of the value of the house on your kitchen, but the right kitchen can add as much as 15 per cent to the asking price of a property for sale.

Do not spend more than 10 per cent of the value of your house on the kitchen because you will not recoup the money. If you are doing up the kitchen to help sell the house, do not spend a lot of money. The chances are that the buyers will rip out your kitchen and put in their own units of choice, so keep the design simple. Buyers hate wasting money. They do not want to spend a lot on a house because it has a new kitchen when they intend to put that kitchen straight on the skip. They will find a cheaper house.

Whatever you do, don't skimp too much on the quality of the units and worktops because this is what will make the kitchen and the house look cheap. If you plan to sell the kitchen appliances with the house, it is often worth spending more on these than on the units because buyers will recognize the brand names and like the idea of buying good-quality washing machines, dishwashers and so on.

Kitchens on a budget

If you do not have as much as 5 per cent of the value of your house to spend, it is better to think creatively rather than to spend the money on a kitchen that is too cheap for the property. Painting old units in fresh, up-to-date colours and putting in new flooring, tiles and light fittings can transform a room for relatively little money if your kitchen is tired but sound.

Changing kitchen doors while leaving existing units in place is often recommended as the budget way to update a kitchen and supposedly add thousands of pounds to the value. This is a fallacy. There is nothing wrong with changing the kitchen doors alone if you don't like the existing ones or as a stopgap option if you cannot immediately afford a new kitchen. But new doors on old kitchen units will not add a penny in value. It is an obvious presentation trick that anyone with half an eye can see through as soon as they open the cupboard doors. And all prospective buyers open cupboard doors.

Locating the kitchen

You should try to create the impression that the kitchen is the heart of the home. An open-plan flat incorporating the kitchen into the living space does this, but if there is insufficient space to open up the kitchen into a living area or if you prefer having the option of keeping the two separate, you should still try to ensure that the kitchen is not cut off or isolated from the rest of the home. Think about using a half-wall, behind which you conceal the sink or the hob, or use a glass wall as a shield so that you can still benefit from through light.

Kitchens no longer need to be tucked away in the back of the house. If you are extending at the back across the width of the house, you could consider putting the kitchen in one of the front reception rooms and turning the back into a large living room that opens on to the garden. Opinions are divided on the wisdom of doing this, however, and it can turn out to be prohibitively expensive.

Planning a kitchen

Remodelling a kitchen can be one of the most difficult projects in the house. It is the most expensive room to equip, and people's taste in cupboards, flooring and appliances is highly personal and fashion-sensitive. There is a bewildering range of choice in both design and price, and the state-of-the-art kitchen that was installed just a few months ago is bound to look dated after five to seven years.

It is all too easy to make mistakes, either by being talked into spending far too much money by persuasive salesmen or by buying something too cheap, which quickly falls apart. Exciting

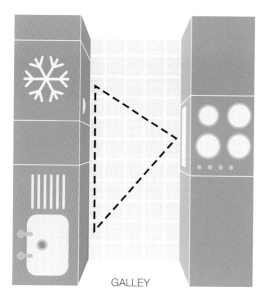

GALLEY

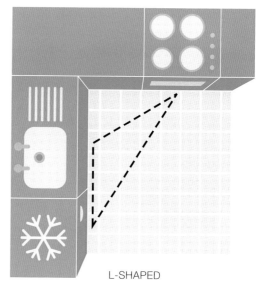

L-SHAPED

Above The most effective use of the space in a kitchen is obtained by arranging the main utilities – the cooker, the refrigerator and sink in a triangle. Even if potential buyers are not aware of the benefit of the triangular arrangement, they will notice that the kitchen looks comfortable to work in.

new technology is enticing and the emphasis on efficient storage solutions is highly seductive, but this can add hundreds of pounds in hidden extras to the cost and it may not be necessary.

The kitchen is the one room in the house where there is greatest need for the careful integration of the essential services. There are usually a large number of electrical appliances and complicated plumbing, while effective lighting and ventilation are the key to making the room both functional and attractive. This is an area where money spent on professional advice from architects, designers or kitchen planners is rarely wasted, and they often help you avoid costly mistakes.

Working through this minefield to a successful outcome depends on good planning at the outset. The best approach is to put questions of budget and design to one side while you work out how the room will be used.

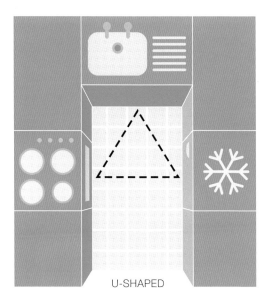

U-SHAPED

Checklist

When you are beginning to plan the kitchen, ask yourself the following questions:

- How many people will use the kitchen every day?
- What is the access to the dining area?
- What is the access to outside? You need to think about both the garden and the front door or wherever the shopping comes into the house – you don't want to carry your weekly groceries or the rubbish too far.
- How does the natural light fall? Does it get morning or afternoon sunshine and which do you want to make the most of?
- How often do you entertain and in what style?
- Will you use the dining area for eating alone or is it also an area for the children to do their homework and somewhere for friends and family to gather for conversation?

Use the checklist on the right to help you decide what specific needs the kitchen must meet.

You need to find the right balance between all your diverse requirements – for storage, for equipment, for cooking space and for living space – in the architecture of the room. Think of knocking rooms together to get additional living space into the kitchen. Ideally, in a house or large flat, there should be room for a dining table to seat eight people and also for a sofa and a TV for the children.

When you are working out the value you can add to the property, the balance has to be appropriate for the potential market for your property when you come to sell. In a family house with three or four bedrooms, the space allocated to the kitchen area and dining area should be approximately 50:50, because families eat and entertain at home regularly. In a flat for young professionals, the kitchen area can be squeezed in favour of providing more living space, because couples with no children tend to eat out more and entertain at home less.

Ventilation

The speedy and effective clearance of cooking smells is especially important when there are no barriers between the kitchen and the living areas. While everyone enjoys the idea of a warm cosy fug of baking cakes, roasting chicken and the old cliché of freshly brewed coffee, no one wants to smell stale cooking fats or boiled vegetables as soon as they step through the front door. Ventilation can either be natural, through windows or doors, or extracted through ducted fans.

Drawing a plan

There are some basic measurements that have to be built into every kitchen plan. These include:

- The standard height of the worktops should be 90cm (36in) off the ground.
- The clearance between the worktop and the bottom of the wall units. This also can vary.
- The size of appliances. American-style double fridges have become increasingly popular, but they will take up more space and thus look out of scale in a small kitchen. There are narrow appliances on the market, and these are suitable for smaller kitchens although they are usually more expensive than the standard width.
- The accessibility of overhead storage units. Standard wall units are either 60cm or 90cm (24in or 36in) tall, but if you have a higher ceiling you can go up. This might look aesthetically appealing but is likely to have limited value in terms of storage as the top levels are usually out of reach unless you stand on a chair.
- The clearance of cupboards and appliance door swings. This needs to be given particular thought in a small or narrow kitchen.

Recycling facilities

As legislation on recycling advances every year and in the next 10 years Britain must increase the percentage of waste it recycles to 30 per cent of the total, households must make their contribution or pay increased charges for garbage collection. You should think about this now when you are installing a new kitchen. Environmental bins, which allow you to sort out your waste, are now routinely supplied by kitchen firms. You might also want to consider installing a food waste-disposal unit.

The triangle

The functional area of a kitchen is divided among three centres of work: preparation and cleaning up of food, cooking and serving, and storage. The sink anchors the preparation area; the cooking area is anchored by the hob and oven and the storage area is centred round the refrigerator. Most designers base their plans on a triangle, an imaginary line linking the three areas. In theory, these areas should not be more than a double arm span apart, but there should always be sufficient space between them so that your movement is not restricted.

Sink

The one immutable rule of kitchen design is that the sink should be sited under the window. This is because the sink tends to be where people spend most time and the position benefits from the natural light. However, with decent lighting under wall units, it is a rule that can be easily broken. If you choose to site your sink along an interior wall amid base units, always leave the space above the sink clear of wall units.

You need the head clearance, it will look better aesthetically and the person who is at the sink won't feel claustrophobic. A wooden drainage rack or some open shelving should fill the gap satisfactorily.

You can also mount the sink on an island unit facing into the room, but this can cause plumbing problems if you cannot get a sufficient downward run on the waste pipe, and does depend on the size of space you have. The other disadvantage of this option is that the island cannot then be used for the hob or range cooker, which allows the cook to face into the living space and to participate in conversation with family and friends.

Dishwasher

It is logical and efficient to site the dishwasher under the worktop next to the sink. It keeps the plumbing neat, and when you are clearing away a meal, you can load the dishwasher or fill the sink with pans without having to walk around the room. Don't skimp on the dishwasher even if you don't use one much yourself. Curiously, this appliance has been slow to win acceptance but is nonetheless regarded as a standard feature by agents when they are valuing a house, and you will lose out if you don't install one. If space is short this is one appliance where you can get away with buying one of the smaller models.

Oven

The position of the oven is less crucial. Eye-level appliances, which save a lot of bending down, are best placed at the end of a run of units. The oven should be close to a work surface so that you can quickly put down an over-hot dish.

Clutter

Kitchens tend to accumulate clutter on the worktops, and most are covered with portable appliances that are in everyday use – the kettle, toaster, coffee grinder, food processor and free-standing microwave. One option to keep them out of sight is to choose a few wall units that have roll-up doors. These cupboards can extend all the way down to the work surface and have power points concealed inside. The appliances can live inside permanently, neatly out of sight when they are not in use.

Choosing a style

There is a huge range of styles available for kitchens, and the choice is personal. But if you want to add value for resale, choose something broadly in keeping with the rest of the property to appeal to future buyers. A traditional farmhouse kitchen would not add much value in an inner-city loft because it would seem out of place, and an industrial, stainless steel, utilitarian kitchen would look odd in a 17th-century rural village house. You also have to think about your potential market.

Other rules of style include not overdoing the number of cupboards. Although it is true that you can never have too much storage space, too many kitchen units will kill the character of a room. Consider buying some free-standing storage, such as an old dresser, on which you can display plates, or installing some glass shelves if you are in a more modern house.

Avoid too many fashionable or gimmicky extras. They have the disadvantages that they can date quickly, that you won't actually use them and that they take up valuable space.

Country

Beloved of women's magazines, the country style, complete with an Aga and a cat snoozing in a rocking chair, is the ultimate in hearth and home fantasies. The units are usually wooden, traditionally pine or oak but more recently cherry or maple. Wooden units are warm and attractive but avoid carved details, because grease clings and they are difficult to clean. This is a look that is less fashionable than it was, particularly in towns, where it is often regarded as too cluttered for today's sleek lines. It still appeals to people who like to be cosy and looks right in some country houses. It works best with terracotta tiles and original wooden floors.

Shaker

The look has been around for 10–15 years and is fashionable in family houses in towns. Its appeal lies in the simple but finely crafted wood fittings. It looks good in Georgian and Victorian houses because it is plain and unfussy and does not detract from the inherent airiness of the rooms. It can be easily updated with new paintwork and handles.

Industrial

This style was made popular with the advent of loft-style living in the mid-1990s. The units often look as if they have come out of the industrial canteens found in factories or in a restaurant. Everything is large and workmanlike. You need a lot of space, and it is not a friendly look. The industrial style is best kept for modern flats in town. The use of stainless steel and glass-fronted fridges has spread into 'softer' kitchens, where it can look good as long as it is used as a

---

Accessories

Accessories to install:

■ A cooker hood is essential in most kitchens.

■ A range cooker is expensive but if there is space, provides efficient heat.

■ Mondo cupboard (a corner cupboard revolving through almost 360 degrees) allows you to store masses of pans and cooking equipment but makes them easily accessible.

Accessories to avoid:

■ Indoor barbecues are too time-consuming to clean thoroughly every time you use them.

■ Round bowl sinks are always far too small, even if you are single.

■ Inset deep-fat fryers emit a smell of stale oil that lingers throughout the house.

---

decorative accent rather than imported *in toto*. Stainless steel is not as easy to maintain as its durability would suggest. It marks easily and shows scratches.

Italian

These are the highly expensive, designer brand names, many of which, but by no means all, come from Italy. You are likely to spend upwards of £30,000. They are characterized by metre-wide units, standing on visible legs, with lots of high-tech gadgets, such as taps that pull out like shower dispensers. The overall look is sleek and modern. The mainstream suppliers will imitate the look in the next few years, but for the moment this is high fashion.

Retro

This is 1950s America, with curvy worktops and large, brightly coloured refrigerators. The emphasis is on fun. It isn't a style that fits well with any period of English architecture, but it can look good in boxy, modern flats and apartments. It may look dated in a few years when fashions change.

Cutting costs without losing value

To keep within your budget, consider some of the following ways to save money.

Kitchen carcasses

The units without the doors are made of veneered chipboard and are fairly similar in construction. There are differences in quality and this is reflected in the price, but many architects are happy to use Ikea or Homebase cupboards and to customize them with expensive door handles and worktops. If you choose this route, make sure you buy units that are neutral in appearance, otherwise the ploy won't work.

Fitting

Skilful joinery can make a cheap kitchen look fantastic. If you can find your own joiner, someone you know and trust to do a good job rather than relying on the kitchen supplier to send you the fitter, you can often save money and get the best return on your investment.

Avoid fashion

A new style of kitchen that is coming into fashion will be available only from top-of-the-range suppliers in the early years. Choose a more classic design that has already found its way into the ranges of the mid-price or budget manufacturers and use accessories to provide the fashionable touches. High-fashion kitchens tend to date quickly, so unless you are planning on selling quickly, they should be avoided. A full stainless steel kitchen, for instance, is already looking very 1990s, but a kitchen with a few stainless steel touches, such as the cooker and the hob, still looks up to date.

Suppliers

If you don't have much experience in renovating kitchens it is easy to go to the big suppliers, which offer free design advice and frequently high levels of discount. Remember, however, that you are paying for their expensive advertising campaigns and their expensive showrooms. Shop around and go to small independent suppliers. They can often offer good value because they do not have the overheads of carrying large stocks and can give a personal service.

Tiles and flooring

There is a huge choice of flooring for kitchens but you need to choose one that will prove hard-wearing, particularly if you have children. Many surfaces described as suitable for kitchens can quickly look tatty. Tiles and flooring give your kitchen an up-to-date look without costing a fortune. See Useful Addresses (pages 193–200) for a list of good suppliers.

Work surfaces

There are four main types of work surface to choose from – laminate, wood, granite and Corian – but you could also consider Formica, slate, concrete or tiles.

- **Laminates** are the cheapest and most common. They consist of woodchip covered in a veneer, and there is a huge choice of colours and patterns. The disadvantage of laminates is that they are not entirely heat-resistant, and once a hot pan has burned the surface, the worktop is ruined. Laminates can also chip easily.
- **Wood** is attractive and warm, and wooden worktops look particularly good in country kitchens. You need to choose a hardwood and avoid the softer options, such as pine. Wood is not a hard-wearing material and is not suitable for a kitchen that is going to suffer wear and tear. It has a tendency to split and then rot if it gets too wet. You also have to maintain wood carefully, oiling the surface regularly to ensure that it does not get marked by hot dishes and pans.
- **Granite** is difficult to fit but is the hardest-wearing surface. It used to be expensive, but the price has fallen significantly in recent years. Shop around and go direct to suppliers to cut your bill further. There is a fairly limited choice of colours and, because this is a natural material, they are all are subject to variation. Granite is heavy and cannot be cut into large pieces, so you will have joins in the surfaces.
- **Corian** is made of reconstituted stone and has the advantages of granite without the weight. Corian is easy to maintain and attractive to look at. The entire work surface can be cut in one piece, and there is a huge choice of colours. It is the most expensive of the four main options.
- **Slate** looks wonderful but can be porous and is too soft for the wear and tear to which it is subjected over a number of years.
- **Marble** is too fragile and porous, although treated marble is sometimes used in expensive kitchens.
- **Concrete** is fashionable in industrial kitchens, and it can look attractive, but it is costly to install.
- **Tiles** can be set into a wooden frame resting on the units. They suffer from a number of disadvantages: they can be easily cracked; they may not be sufficiently heat resistant; and the grouting will stain and look grubby in time.
- **Stainless steel** is fashionable and hard wearing, but is prone to watermarks and needs careful cleaning. Abrasive products will scratch and dull the finish.

Appliances

For a rental property, or if you intend to sell the appliance with a home, you can save money by buying cheaper appliances, but you will probably lose value in proportion. Prospective buyers know the value of brand names and are happy to pay more for good-quality names. In addition, this route is only a short-term saving. The more expensive brands tend to be more reliable and in the long term work out cheaper because you won't have to use the service centres with their astronomical call-out charges so often.

Installing the kitchen

You can use a carpenter to build your kitchen. If you choose to do this, you will probably have to handle the design and supply of materials yourself while the carpenter works to a copy of your specification. It can be cheaper than buying from a retailer, but you might not end up with quite the look you wanted.

You can buy from a kitchen retailer, who will usually supply fitters who remove the old kitchen and fit the new one. This removes a considerable burden of work from your shoulders, but it can be hard to get redress if you are not satisfied with the quality of the workmanship.

An architect will design a bespoke kitchen for you. This is an expensive option, because their fee has to be included in the cost of the project, but if you want something different, this is probably the best route. They will usually find the workmen to fit the kitchen for you as part of their service, and it is worth considering this route if you are undertaking a much larger renovation project.

Kitchen floors

Ideal surfaces:

- **Ceramic tiles** can be cold underfoot but they are practicable and long lasting and are brilliant with underfloor heating.
- **Wooden floors** as long as you don't have children and as long as the wood is hard-wearing, such as oak or iroko; avoid pear or cherry wood, which are soft and scratch easily.
- **Vinyl or linoleum** is durable, hard-wearing and inexpensive, and there is a huge choice of styles.
- **Cork tiles** are currently unfashionable but they are warm and reasonably hard-wearing.

Materials to avoid:

- **Wooden laminate flooring** marks easily and swells and rises if it gets wet.
- **Coir and sisal matting** is a trap for crumbs, vegetables peelings and dog fleas.
- **Sanded floorboards** don't react well to water, and food will get trapped between the cracks.
- **Natural limestone or slate** needs sealing every year, or it stains badly.
- **Moulded resins** show every mark.
- **Carpet** is too impractical in an area where there are likely to be regular spills.
- **Concrete** is simple and cheap, but everything you drop will break as it is so hard. It also needs sealing carefully or it will stain.

Small kitchens

Many converted flats have tiny kitchens, which have been squeezed into cupboards under stairs or into tiny back extensions in order not to compromise the limited living space. There are a number of tricks that interior designers use to improve the efficiency of these small areas and to enhance the illusion of space.

As far as possible, everything should be fitted and kept out of sight. You can install pull-down tables and ironing boards. Use floor-to-ceiling cupboards to maximize storage space. Buy slim-line dishwashers and washing machines to fit in more appliances than would otherwise be possible. Ovens that combine a microwave with a conventional oven also save space while maximizing function.

Keep the colours simple. Use white and stainless steel to reflect the light as much as possible, which will make the space look bigger.

Utility areas

The utility area has traditionally been found in the kitchen, particularly in small houses or flats where there is no space for a separate room. You will add more value to your property if you can remove the washing machine from the cooking area. If you can, use a cupboard under the stairs or steal space from the bathroom to make a cupboard large enough to install a machine and dryer.

If that is not a viable option and the kitchen is the only place to put the washing machine, make sure that it is as far from the cooker and the hob as possible. Usually it will be placed close to the sink and dishwasher to ensure efficiency of plumbing.

Dining

Separate formal dining rooms are a thing of the past except in large, grand houses. The dining area now forms part of the kitchen, which is usually the most practical use of space in the house while the old dining room is used as a TV and playroom or study. Even if you retain a separate dining room, you should make space in the kitchen for eating quick meals and snacks. If your kitchen if not big enough for a full-scale dining table, buy a small round table with two chairs for breakfast and cosy suppers. It is always a helpful selling point.

The dining area in the kitchen should be clearly demarcated from the functional cooking space. This is the area for relaxing and socializing with family and friends and should not be utilitarian in feel. The space should be adaptable for both formal and informal occasions, for a hurried breakfast or a leisurely dinner party.

Use lighting, different colours on the walls and different flooring materials to separate kitchen and dining areas. Create the sense of a focal point around the dining table by the use of a low hanging central light. You can add sofas and TVs to create the atmosphere of an informal family room but you will need a large space so not to overcrowd the room.

The shape of the room will dictate the shape of your dining table. Round dining tables are considered more sociable than rectangular ones. If you regularly cater for groups of more than six, the proportion of a rectangular table is easier to live with than a round table. Table linen allows you to dress a table up or down as suits the occasion.

Summary: The Kitchen

- This is the most important room when it comes to adding value to a property and one of the most difficult projects to undertake.
- How well a kitchen functions as a living space and a practical working place determines how much value it can add and a good kitchen will often clinch the deal for a buyer.
- Spend 5 per cent (but no more than 10 per cent) of the property's value on the kitchen; the right kitchen can add as much as 15 per cent to the asking price.
- If your budget is tight, paint old units and put in new flooring, tiles and light fittings. New cupboard doors will not add value, but it is often worth spending money on quality appliances if you plan to sell them with the house.

Planning

- Success depends on good planning from the outset. Money spent on professional advice from architects, designers and kitchen planners is rarely wasted.
- First work out how the room will be used considering the diverse requirements for storage, equipment, cooking space and living space.
- The balance of kitchen to dining/living space must be appropriate for the potential market for your property when you come to sell.
- To add value for resale, choose a style in keeping with the rest of the property.
- Avoid fashionable gimmicky extras and having too many units (which kills character).
- You will add value to your property if you can remove the washing machine from the cooking area.

⑫ The Bathroom

Our ideas about the function of bathrooms have undergone a revolution in the last 10 years. No longer just a place to promote cleanliness, a bathroom is now seen as a luxury retreat from the stresses of the outside world and the centre for well-being in the home.

Adding a bathroom

The idea that cleanliness is next to godliness is a quite recent one – the Elizabethans, for instance, thought one bath a year quite sufficient. It was the Victorian middle classes who promoted the benefits of scrubbing and regular washing at a time when running water in domestic houses became readily available and the importance of hygiene in preventing disease was first understood. Public baths were then considered acceptable, as they had been in the days of the Romans. But when the only option for many people was an outdoor lavatory and a tin bath in front of the fire, an internal bathroom to promote cleanliness became a status symbol.

Throughout the 20th century the bathroom was a place to demonstrate material wealth in accordance with the fashions of the day. The gold taps and whirlpool corner baths of the 1970s and 1980s succeeded the coloured suites of the 1950s and 1960s. In the last 10 years the therapeutic role of the bathroom has come into focus, accompanying the rise of spa centres and relaxation treatments. For women burdened with busy jobs and noisy, demanding children, the bathroom is the one room in the house they can call their own. The bathroom is a sanctuary.

The desire for privacy in this most personal of rooms has led to an increased demand for individual bathrooms in a house. Even in two-bedroom flats, it is becoming standard to fit two *en-suite* bathrooms or, if space is limited, shower rooms. In a family house estate agents look for a family bathroom, an *en-suite* bathroom to accompany the master bedroom and, preferably, a downstairs cloakroom for guests. The ratio of bedrooms to bathrooms should be 2:1 and certainly no more than 3:1. Many people now want a house where every bedroom has its own bathroom.

Refurbishment costs

In terms of financial outlay remodelling a bathroom need not be that expensive. If the basic suite is sound, new taps, tiles, lighting and flooring can achieve a swift transformation, which will certainly make it more saleable. Nothing is more depressing when house hunting than a grungy bath with the taps caked in limestone, water stains down the enamel and tile grouting that has turned black with mould. Estate agents say the bathroom is hugely important in helping to sell a house and that you can make as much as £10,000–£15,000 extra with a swanky bathroom. One survey said that an extra bathroom could add up to 10 per cent to the value of the house, although it does depend on the type of property.

The main cost of refitting a bathroom is the plumbing and fitting work, and ideally you should get several quotes. The best route is to get a word-of-mouth recommendation from someone who has used them: plumbers tend to respond better to such an approach than to a cold call.

You can refurbish a bathroom for about £1,500, including plumbing, if you shop around, but this will be rather basic in style and quality. To install a bathroom that will last a few years, you should increase your budget to around £5,000. The cost of the tiles can vary hugely, and if you choose expensive ones you will add considerably to the total budget. If you include air baths, steam rooms and expensive taps you could easily run up a much bigger bill. If you spend more than £10,000 you are unlikely to recoup your investment.

Adding value

To add extra value to your house rather than just recouping your costs by modernizing the bathrooms, you should consider moving the bathroom if necessary so that it is located in a convenient space near to the bedrooms. In many Victorian houses, which were originally not built with bathrooms, developers installed them wherever they could find a convenient small space, and if that was downstairs in the basement off the kitchen, that was where it went. House buyers hate downstairs bathrooms except as facilities for guests.

Another way to add extra value is to divide an over-large bathroom into two, creating an *en suite* shower room for one of the bedrooms. In the 1920s and 1930s many houses were built with small bathrooms and separate, rather gloomy lavatories in an adjacent small room. Knocking these two rooms together and, if necessary, stealing extra space from the landing area can give you a much more attractive room, which will be large enough for a separate shower cubicle.

To make more efficient use of the space in an existing bathroom, consider replacing some of the fittings with smaller models, which will make it look bigger and provide more usable floor space, where you can install storage for linen and toiletries.

If you have to sacrifice a bedroom to get an extra bathroom, think again. You will reduce the value of a four-bedroom house with one bathroom if you turn it into a three-bedroom house with two bathrooms, but a six-bedroom house will probably be improved in value if it is turned into five bedrooms and two bathrooms.

Planning a bathroom

Although bathrooms may be used for luxurious self-indulgence, planning a new bathroom is all about practicalities. Is this a family bathroom that will be busy, with several people crowding in early in the day? If so, the materials used should be practicable and child friendly. You need to have non-slip flooring and basins with curved edges, so that a small child is less likely to cut his head open if he bangs it against the basin, and the taps should be easy for small hands to use.

The first stage, therefore, is to start by thinking carefully about who will use the bathroom and given that, what the optimum use of space might be. Two basins, for instance, are useful in a family bathroom but are probably wasted in a more private *en suite*.

When you are planning the refurbishment of a bathroom pay attention first to the existing plumbing supply and waste outlets. These are permanent fixtures and cannot be easily changed. In particular, the soil stack, which serves the lavatory, is expensive to move and, if possible, you should plan your new layout around this remaining where it is.

The other main consideration when it comes to layout is that, with the exception of *en-suite* bathrooms, the room should be accessible from a common space. No one wants to be woken in the night by someone going through their bedroom to get to the bathroom.

Architecturally, bathroom spaces can start out as some of the least attractive in the house as they are squeezed out of otherwise redundant spaces, such as old attics in the roof or the former boxroom. The spaces are frequently windowless and too small. The saving grace of such rooms is that a bathroom can use space more efficiently than any other room, and alcoves can be transformed into storage, allowing maximum use of a limited floor area.

Drawing a floorplan

The simplest way to plan a redesign is to draw up a floor plan. You need to install a minimum of three pieces – a bath or shower, a lavatory and a basin. Of these, the basin will get maximum use, so it should be placed nearest the door. The bath and lavatory can be more private – sited round an awkward corner, for instance. You need to calculate not just the space each of these appliances will take up but also to make sure that there is enough floor space around each of them. A bath needs its own floor space so that you can manoeuvre comfortably around it. You need enough space in front of a basin to bend over to wash and enough space in front of the lavatory for your knees not to be pushed up against something else.

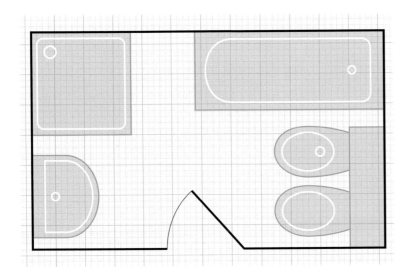

Left Having a shower cubicle in a bathroom or a separate *en-suite* shower or bathroom can be a strong selling point for busy couples. When designing a bathroom, it is important to make sure that it is practical as well as stylish. Buyers will be put off by such details as the handbasin being too close to the door.

Ideally the door should open inwards into the bathroom, but if space is really restricted, you can consider having it open outwards. Take care that you do not create a blockage on a landing by having the door opening outwards, because this may well constitute a fire hazard and be in breach of building regulations. The other decision in a small space is whether to install an under-sized bath or make do with a shower. If this is the only bathroom, it is probably better to go with the small bath and an overhead shower, but you have more flexibility if this is the second bathroom.

While most people grapple with under-sized bathrooms, there can be just as many problems where space is not an issue. If a larger bedroom has been converted into the main bathroom, it can look rather forbidding to have all the appliances round the walls. It is better in these circumstances to consider a free-standing bath in the middle of the room.

Choosing a layout

Fixtures can be arranged with the plumbing installed on one, two or three walls of the bathroom – these are known as 'wet walls' – and your decision on which to choose will be determined to some extent by the position of the door and windows. One wet wall is the cheapest to install but limits the design possibilities. Two wet walls should give you more floor space and is the design to choose if the door opens into the middle of the room. Three wet walls are usually only suitable for larger spaces.

You also need to decide if you are going to conceal much of the pipework and lavatory cistern behind walls and plaster. Remember in your planning that you must have easy access in case you need to have the cistern repaired, and you also need to install stopcocks so that you can easily turn off the water supply to each individual appliance.

Fittings

The vexed question of colour is the first issue to deal with. Coloured bathroom suites have been out of fashion for 20 years, so they are probably due for a revival, but if you want to play it safe, you should choose a white suite.

Some variation has crept in through the back door. Glass basins have become fashionable in the last few years and the fashion for reconstituted stone and limestone has seen the use of these materials in baths. The vogue for stainless steel has spread from the kitchen to the bathroom where it is used for basins and lavatories, but this trend is probably limited to modernistic lofts in urban locations. Unusual materials tend to come with a hefty price tag.

Lavatories

There are two types of lavatory on the market: the cistern type and the syphonic type. The cistern system is the old-fashioned, overhead placement, which washes water down and the pressure of the fall is enough to wash away the contents of the bowl. It leaves the pipework exposed, which, unless you are re-creating a period bathroom, is not particularly attractive. Overhead cisterns have largely been superseded by the close-coupled system, which is more attractive in appearance but water pressure can sometimes be inadequate.

The syphonic system, where the bowl and tank are in one piece, is quieter and more efficient but also more expensive.

Lavatories in conversions Macerators have become available in recent years. These break down waste matter so that it can be carried away down a narrow 38mm (1½in) pipe to join the soil pipe. These are useful in bathrooms that are being carved out of internal space where linking the lavatory to the soil pipe is impracticable. They do however have some disadvantages. You have to take great care with what goes down the lavatory – only paper is allowed, or the pipe will get blocked. This makes them unsuitable for family bathrooms and probably also for guest facilities, because you won't be able to guarantee that other people will respect your instructions on usage. They also can be noisy and irritating to live with. Their use is probably best confined to small *en-suite* rooms that aren't much used.

Basins

Basins traditionally come in pedestal or cantilevered styles. There are also basins that are designed to be set into a cabinet, which can solve many of your storage problems at a stroke and conceal plumbing pipes. In recent years basins shaped like large fruit bowls standing on wooden shelves have become popular; these are usually served by wall-mounted plumbing pipes (rather than pipes rising from the floor), which makes them more expensive to install.

Baths

Baths are available for as little as £150, but for this you will only get one made of acrylic. These come in a wide range of colours, styles and sizes. They are lightweight and affordable.

It is worth spending more to get a bath made of pressed steel. This is rigid and tough but tends to be cold to touch, although this will not be a problem as long as the bathroom itself is warm.

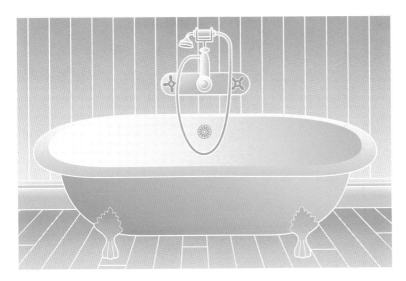

Left A traditional Victorian- or Edwardian-style pedestal bath makes an attractive addition to a period bathroom. Reclaimed examples can be found in salvage yards and specialists can re-enamel them if needed.

Cast-iron baths are the most durable but are heavy, which might make them unsuitable on upstairs floors. They are the most expensive and are not suitable for small flats. If you have inherited a cast-iron bath that is looking past its best, you should get it re-enamelled. This will save you the expense of getting it taken out, when it usually has to be broken into pieces.

Whirlpool or Jacuzzi-style baths are still popular but have an image problem. Only install one of these if you personally enjoy it. The extra cost will not add value to your property. On the other hand, Edwardian-style roll-top baths are popular and add a touch of luxury; reproduction models are cheaply available.

Showers

As working hours have got longer, the popularity of showers has increased. The power shower is now an essential if you want to add the 'wow' factor to your bathroom.

A power shower has a pump installed between it and the water supply to increase the pressure to give you that energizing boost rather than the sad dribble that comes out of shower attachments to bath taps. There are many types of pump on the market, and some have to be sited in specific places, which is particularly important if your hot-water tank is several floors away from the shower. Seek expert advice before you buy and make sure that the retailer will be willing to exchange the goods if you do not buy the right type of pump.

Where space is limited the shower may have to be installed over the bath with a glass screen door or curtain to protect the floor, but a separate shower cubicle is much more satisfactory. If you have a small second bathroom, consider removing the bath and making it a shower room. A downstairs bathroom can be converted so that the shower can be used for someone coming in after sport.

Right Stylish, modern fittings are available for the more contemporary bathroom. While this handbasin would not be appropriate for a Victorian family bathroom, it may add value to a modern home, especially if teamed up with an equally modern bath and contemporary fittings.

Installing a shower tray requires care so that the tray does not move when under pressure from body weight and water and cause leaks. The wall tiles should come to rest on top of the tray, not run down the back of it, to help create a proper seal. The drain should have a trap that is at least 8cm (3in) wide so that the water soaks away quickly enough.

Taps

Frequently much more expensive than ceramic bathroom fittings, the taps are the fashion statement of the room. There is a huge range at every price level, and by and large you will get what you pay for: well-made taps cost more but stand up to the rigours of hard water and limestone deposits much better than less expensive ones. Try to pick a style that matches the rest of the house and the bathroom fittings.

Mixer taps for both the sink and the bath are preferable because you will never end up scalding yourself on the hot water, but you must make sure that the water pressure from both the hot and cold taps is about even or they will not work well. You should have a shower attachment fitted on the bath tap even if there is an overhead shower installed because it is always useful for washing hair or simply cleaning the bath, and this can be added relatively easily and cheaply.

You can mount the taps on the bath or basin or on the wall, but make sure you have the right suite to do so. Wall-mounted taps free space around the bath, but they are more trouble to maintain. If the washer goes, for instance, you can have a leak behind the wall for months without knowing until the tiles start bulging and you notice problems with damp.

Several brands have emerged at the top of the market in the same way as there are star brands in kitchen appliances. Once installed, however, they are less easily recognizable than a top-of-the-range oven or refrigerator, so it is arguable whether they actually add value other than in extremely expensive properties. If you enjoy something really well made and plan to stay in the property for some years, the expenditure may be worth it.

Storage

Bottles of bath oil, scented candles and cosmetics displayed at the back of the bath look alluring in shops, but it somehow never looks quite the same at home. A small collection suddenly grows into a mountain of clutter, some of it covered in dust because it is so rarely used. There are also bottles of bleach, spare lavatory rolls and medical supplies, which never look good on display. So you need to leave space to build in shelves where everything can be tucked away out of sight. There is also plenty of choice for free-standing storage in bathroom shops.

Wet rooms

Wet rooms have become increasingly popular, especially in upmarket new developments, and they are useful where space is limited. In effect, having a wet room involves turning the whole bathroom into a shower. You install a giant showerhead and enjoy the strong water pressure. The floor slopes so that the water drains away into a plughole at the lowest point. You must make sure that they are properly installed and that the tiles are laid on the correct foundations of marine ply or Venetian wet

plaster. Plasterboard should not be used behind tiles in a wet room because it becomes porous if there are any leaks and is difficult and therefore expensive to remove.

Make sure that the ventilation is adequate. In the damp English climate, the walls of a wet room can take a long time to dry off and there is nothing more unappealing than a bathroom where the water puddles on the floor.

Steam cabins

These small cubicles can be installed with a shower to allow two people to sit and enjoy a relaxing steam. You will need specialist advice on the installation to ensure that the cabin is properly sealed, otherwise you will be creating condensation problems in the house. Estate agents report that steam cabins are popular with buyers, but how much they are actually used is uncertain.

Lighting and ventilation

Lighting in bathrooms needs careful consideration. You need strong, bright light for applying make-up or shaving, but you also need to be able to create a softer, more subdued light for relaxing in the bath. Bathroom lights are subject to greater regulation than lighting elsewhere in the house because the combination of water and electricity can be dangerous. Always ask the retailer if the light fittings you are choosing are designated as suitable for bathrooms.

Halogen downlighters are successful in bathrooms because the bright light compensates for the darkness or limited light found in many bathrooms. Keep candles for the relaxing times and think about installing additional task lights above the sink or mirror (see page 153).

An extractor fan is always a good idea because it cuts down on condensation and is, in any case, a legal requirement in an internal bathroom. The fan must be wired through the light switch, which itself has to be operated on a pull cord or located outside the bathroom door.

Heating

Most bathrooms are small and can be kept warm sufficiently with a heated towel rail. These can be run on gas or electricity and come in a range of attractive designs. Older properties might have electric heaters, installed above head height in order to prevent any risk of contact with water.

Decoration

Steam and condensation mean that bathroom decorations have to be water-resistant. You should use eggshell or gloss, if you want to be bold, but emulsion paint is not suitable.

Floor-to-ceiling tiling offers a better option. There is nothing better for water resistance, tiles are easy to clean and maintain and they are much more durable than paint. They also help make a small space look bigger. There has been an explosion in colours and styles of tiles in recent years, and it need not be expensive to tile a bathroom throughout. For a flat that may be rented out to tenants, for instance, you can choose the cheapest white ceramic tiles and break them up with a rope border or mosaic band. It will always look clean, fresh and bright no matter what they do to the rest of the flat.

The current fashion is for mosaic tiles or limestone finishes. The ceramic copies are better than the real thing, because not only are they much cheaper, but they do not need sealing every year. Painted tongue-and-groove panelling is also popular, particularly in Scotland, because it takes the chill out of the room.

Mirrors are essential in a bathroom and can be used to create an illusion of space in a small, internal room. It is best to restrict the glass to one wall, however, because too many unwanted reflections are not always flattering.

The floor covering must be water-resistant, and, as in the kitchen, ceramic tiles, linoleum and vinyl are the best options. To beat the chill in a bathroom, install underfloor heating.

Colour

Even if the bathroom suite is white, you do not have to banish colour entirely from the bathroom. Colour can create illusions of space and atmosphere, so in a room that is small it has a particularly important function. You can, for example, use two contrasting or complementary colours in the one room to draw attention away from its awkward shape.

Pale shades make a room look larger, while darker shades will make it look smaller. Using similar tones for all the surfaces will also make the room look more spacious. Natural light affects colour in a room. North-facing rooms, for example, tend to be chillier, so it is best to avoid the cooler colours, but you will have more choice in sunnier, south-facing rooms.

If you are refurbishing your house with an eye to resale, you should choose colours that will not put off potential buyers. Blue is always a safe choice in a bathroom because it has traditional associations with water and swimming pools and helps to create a relaxing, calm atmosphere. Neutral colours are also popular in bathrooms and mix well with white. You can choose from soft creams, beige, pebble, mushroom and oatmeal. These colours achieve softness but at the same time look stylish and chic. Add some texture through natural stone tiles or wood to stop the scheme becoming too bland. These are not ideal schemes for bathrooms that are used by young children because they will get dirty too quickly.

If you want to add a more dramatic effect do this through the furnishings, such as the towels and bathmats. These can be easily changed if you get tired of the colour or if you are looking to create a more neutral look when you sell.

Summary: The Bathroom

There is an increased demand for individual bathrooms, now seen as luxury retreats.

Adding value

- The bathroom is very important in helping to sell a property: stylish bathrooms can add £10,000–£15,000 extra.
- If the basic suite is sound, new taps, tiles, lighting and flooring can achieve a swift transformation to make it more saleable.
- The main cost is the plumbing and fitting work; ideally get several quotes.
- Try to plan your new layout around the existing plumbing supply and waste outlet.
- Consider moving the bathroom to a more convenient location, e.g. nearer the bedrooms.
- Divide an over-large bathroom into a bathroom and an en-suite shower room.
- Think carefully before sacrificing a bedroom to make an extra bathroom.

Planning

- Who will use the bathroom and what will make best use of the space?
- Unless en-suite, the bathroom should be accessible from common space.
- Draw up a floor plan to decide on the best arrangement of appliances and to check there is sufficient space around each one.
- White is still the safest choice for the suite. Unusual materials (e.g. limestone) are usually expensive.
- A separate shower cubicle is preferable to an over-bath shower if you have space.
- Taps are the fashion statement; the range is huge and generally you get what you pay for.
- Light fittings must be suitable for use in bathrooms.
- Floor-to-ceiling tiles are better than paint. Never use emulsion paint.

 Living Rooms

The largest rooms in the house will probably be the ones you spend least time on refurbishing, but don't underestimate the impact on potential purchasers that thoughtfully presented, comfortable rooms will have and how much their decision will be swayed by the appearance of these rooms. The main reception room will be the first room that many potential buyers will see, so it is worth spending time and money to get it looking right.

Reception rooms

If the kitchen is now the family living room, the living room has become the formal playroom, and it can be both a space for children to play and somewhere for adults to relax and entertain. Nevertheless, it retains some of the status display symbols of the old-fashioned parlour, the most public room in the house, where the best paintings and furniture are displayed. The danger is that these functions become contradictory, and the result is so stylistically confusing that the room always looks a mess. Balancing conflicting functions is the key to adding value in one of the most important rooms in the house.

When they are viewing a house, buyers will look at the reception room first to see how it fulfils its public status as the space for entertainment, but they also want somewhere that is warm and inviting. The aim, therefore, should not be to go for a perfect style, which is often chilling in atmosphere, nor to make a fashion statement as seen in magazines, which will quickly acquire a clichéd feel and is usually inappropriate for an individual's needs. Instead, remember that a living room needs a structure to marry its different functions. This should not be confused with a theme, which sadly happens all too often and looks out of place. Begin by asking the questions listed on the right to identify how you are going to use the room.

If you live in a typical Victorian or Edwardian terraced house you may have a reception room that was originally two rooms that have been knocked through. Although this has the advantage of bringing light in from both ends of the room, there are substantial drawbacks to this arrangement. You never quite conquer the sense that these are two separate rooms, and the space rarely functions as a coherent whole. The room is inevitably long and narrow, and most social functions will end up with people congregating at one end or the other. If you try to widen the room by knocking out the wall with the hall you can destroy the architectural integrity of the house, so this doesn't work effectively either.

The solution is to install dividing doors, which can be folded out when you need to open the space up but that you can keep closed so that you can devote each room to a separate function, say a formal sitting room for adults and a playroom for the children. Check with your local authority that any work you do conforms to current building regulations.

Seating

No matter how a reception room is used, the essence of the room is a comfortable sofa or two and surrounding chairs to create the centre.

Key questions on use

- Will the room be used primarily for entertaining? If so, should the television be somewhere else?
- Will it be the family room where children will need space to play?
- How can you create an atmosphere of calm and comfort?

Seating affects behaviour. A hard, straight-backed sofa will impart a feeling of formality, while a large, squashy one will suggest a more relaxed atmosphere. How close you place the sofa and chairs to each other will determine how you and your guests socialize. A mixture of seating, such as a clean, modern sofa set against a stylish carved antique chair, will help to create a sense of individual style. When there are guests, remember that a two-seater sofa will only accommodate one person comfortably, and a three-seater sofa will only seat two people, so leave plenty of room for people not to feel crowded.

Seating is usually grouped around a focal point, such as a fireplace, while in modern homes the coffee table often forms the central nexus. It can also be used to zone a room into its different functions.

If the major problem you face is lack of space – or the inefficient use of space – consider how you can modify or rearrange it. The emphasis should be on creating a quality space and the most comfortable room setting for you. Remove any unnecessary pieces of furniture and use pieces whose scale fits the size of the room. Consider using multi-functional furniture, such as a seat that contains storage. Foldable furniture or built-in furniture tailored to the size and shape of the room can help to reduce space problems.

Recreation

In the post-war period the focal point of a reception room was the television, which was also a status symbol. These days it is not a good idea to make the television the focal point of a room because not everyone wants to sit and watch it. It is better positioned in a corner away from the conversational centre. Better still, if you have the space, it should be moved away from the reception room altogether into a separate media room, which can accommodate a large, flat screen and family computers.

Music systems are another essential part of the entertainment function of the reception room. Most systems are modern and functional in appearance, so they cause little visual disturbance, but if you can get the cables under the floorboards, you will improve the appearance of the room. For a state-of-the-art system connected up to a central computerized hub, which serves the whole house, you will need to contact a specialist retailer at the start of the refurbishment programme so that the wiring can be put in place at an early stage.

Storage

Clutter should be avoided at all costs. It makes a room look smaller and a house less well cared for. Videos, CDs, drinks and games should all be stored away. You can buy attractive modern storage cupboards in furniture shops or you can have cupboards built in. Obvious places to site cupboards are in recesses on either side of the chimney breast. The most attractive are low cupboards built to dado height with shelves above, but do not take the shelves all the way up to the ceiling because it gives a DIY feel. If you have a bay, cupboards built under a windowseat are ideal for concealing toys and children's clutter.

The cupboards should be made of wood or MDF painted to match the walls of the room. Metallic or industrial shelving can also look good if it teams with the style of the rest of the room. Glass shelving look can look great displaying anything from rough and rustic objects to fine porcelain figurines; again it depends on the style of the house.

Focal points

This is a phrase much loved by estate agents, who complain that a room does not come together unless there is a focal point to centre around and pull together all the disparate elements.

Traditionally, the fireplace has been regarded as the hearth and heart of the home. In a period house this remains the case, and you should think about reinstating a period fireplace if it has been removed. Some people still love an open fire, particularly if they live in the country, but you will need to check that the chimney is still in working condition. If the chimney needs relining or has been capped at some point in the past, reinstating it will be expensive. You probably will not get your money back, although it is worth doing for your own enjoyment. A cheaper option is to install a real gas fire, which requires only a simple flue outlet.

Many people, especially in towns, do not want to be bothered with the work of cleaning out the ashes or dealing with the dirt from a real fire. Period fireplaces can look attractive if the hearth is filled with plants or flowers. This lacks the warmth of a real fireplace, so make sure the mantelpiece is filled with interesting objects.

Studies and home offices

The advent of the PC, broadband and attendant technology has revolutionized home working in the last 20 years. For many people work and leisure are now based under one roof, and home working is especially suitable for people involved in media, design and creative work. Using the dining room table in the day is no longer acceptable, however, and more than ever, the worker must have a room of their own.

A home office *per se* will not add that much value to your home because it is not that expensive to convert a suitable room, but it will make the house more saleable because buyers now expect to find a corner where wiring is in place and some shelving provided as the designated place for the computer.

If your work is of the kind that involves receiving clients at home, you need to ensure privacy for both the clients and the family. The ideal arrangement is for you to work in a room to which you can take visitors without having to lead them through the main body of the house, and it should be clear from the way the room is furnished that this is a professional environment and separate from domestic life. Your clients should not have to witness the mound of clothes waiting to be ironed or glimpse the unmade beds behind half-open doors.

The best solution is to convert a spare bedroom into an office space, but if that is not possible, part of the hall or the space under the stairs can be annexed. If you have the luxury of space and can exercise a choice about where to work, you should select a room that is quiet and away from the main bustle of the house. You also need a well-lit room, preferably with good natural light from a window, and, even better, it should enjoy a window with a good view over the garden.

If you need to combine your office with a bedroom that is used for guests, it is essential that you should be able to pack away your papers easily. Good storage is vital in these circumstances, but you might consider having some special cupboards built to make the equipment disappear altogether when necessary. Because the bedroom function will be redundant most of the time, you should consider buying a sofa bed so that it does not dominate the room when you are working.

The final option is the garden shed. This provides a sense of separateness from domestic life, which can help to improve concentration. You need to insulate it properly so that it is warm and cosy in winter, and to run separate telephone lines so that communication is not made difficult for anyone in the house.

Bedrooms

The bedroom is where we spend most of our lives at home, but they are neglected rooms, full of clutter and with overflowing cupboards.

A bedroom is also the most personal room in the house on which we stamp our identity. There are, however, some essential guidelines to follow if you want to make sure that you add the maximum value to your property.

The ideal bedroom is one that looks like a calming sanctuary, where you would be happy to spend an hour reading a book in peace and quiet as well as sleeping.

The master bedroom is the most important of the bedrooms. It should be upstairs and have easy access to the bathroom or, preferably, have an *en-suite* bathroom. There should also be fitted cupboards that offer plenty of storage, especially if the room is an awkward shape and it is difficult to find suitable furniture.

Although Americans believe that you can never have enough closets, cupboards can be too much of a good thing if they unbalance the shape of the room. Always respect the style and period of the property when you are designing or buying cupboards.

If you choose to buy fitted cupboards from one of the many retail suppliers, a representative from the company will usually pay a site visit and work out with you the internal design of the cupboards to suit your needs. You can choose what height you want the wardrobe rail to be, how much shelving you need and how it should be organized, where mirrors and internal lighting should be positioned and what type of handles you want. They will measure up, draw plans and install the furniture.

You can get a similar service from a joiner, although you may have to undertake some of the initial design work yourself. The cost will vary depending on the quality of the wood you want

to use. Whatever your approach avoid the DIY look at all costs; it will detract from the value of the house.

Choosing a style

Style in a bedroom is highly personal and can easily be varied by a change of bed linen and curtains. You should try to avoid an over-feminine look, which can be unappealing to any men thinking of buying your home. Keep to plain unfussy furnishings. In rural locations, where the views from the house can be the main attraction, simplicity should be the keynote.

The bed is the focus around which the style of the room will be defined. A draped four-poster bed, even a modern, simple one, will make a room look smaller. If you want to maximize the feeling of space, choose a plain simple headboard and paint the walls the same colour.

Usually, the space will work best if the bed is placed with a head against the wall rather than being against the window or standing alone in the centre of the room. But it does depend on the room. In bedrooms with high ceilings, a bed standing alone in the middle of the room can look dramatic. Place the bed where the space around it is easily negotiated – a double bed in a corner of the room is awkward if one person has to climb over the other every night.

If the bedroom has to double as a study, make sure that the workspace is clearly defined and limited to one portion of the room. If you are living in a studio where the bedroom doubles as a sitting room during the day, try to fold away or conceal the bed in a cupboard. Installing a mezzanine can also increase the use of space in a confined area, but make sure that there is enough space to stand up and move around on the upper floor, otherwise it is likely to detract rather than add value.

It would be a mistake to believe that decorating a child's bedroom around a theme adds value to a property. The danger is that buyers may actively dislike your ideas and be put off, or they may want to use the room for a completely separate function or their children may be a different age. The safest option is simply to keep the colours cheerful and design a theme that is based on the furniture in the room rather than the decoration.

Summary: Living Rooms

Well-presented, comfortable living rooms can make a big impact on potential buyers, so it is worth spending time and money to get it right.

Reception rooms

- The main reception room is often the first room potential buyers see. Balancing the conflicting functions of public display room and family playroom is the key to adding value.
- The emphasis should be on creating a quality space that works for you.
- Don't make the television a focal point.
- Avoid clutter: it makes a room look smaller and the house less well cared for.
- Reinstating a chimney and fireplace is expensive and you're unlikely to get your money back.
- New technology means that many people now work from home. A home office will not add value to your home, but will make it more saleable.

Bedrooms

- These most personal rooms, where we spend most of our time at home, are often neglected and cluttered.
- Plenty of storage is essential. If a room is an awkward shape, fitted cupboards are ideal, but be careful that they don't unbalance the room.
- Always respect the style and period of the property when designing or buying cupboards.
- The DIY look will detract from the value of the house.
- The master bedroom should have good access to a bathroom, preferably an *en suite*.
- When trying to sell, keep to plain, unfussy furnishings and avoid an over-feminine style. Make it look and feel like a calming sanctuary.
- Decorating a child's bedroom around a theme does not add value.

⑭ Decorating

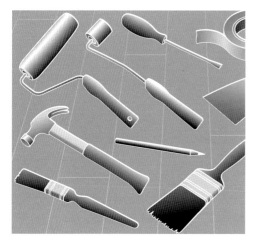

When the major work of installing the new kitchen and bathroom and building the understair cupboards is complete, you can turn to the more enjoyable work of decorating your property and adding the details that turn a house into a home. Choosing a colour is always a personal, subjective decision, but beware of going to the extreme of painting everywhere white. You want potential purchasers to see a comfortable, inviting home.

Lighting

You should aim to install lighting that allows you to vary it according to the time of day and the atmosphere you want to create. You need bright, concentrated light for working areas, such as the study and the kitchen, but softer tones in living areas. Even better is to be able to manipulate the light in most rooms so that you can dim and brighten different corners, create shadows to emphasize focal points and affect the colours.

The limitations of the traditional central pendant lights with their harsh overhead glare have long been recognized, but the scope of lighting domestic interiors has been transformed by technology and today's lighting is driven by the fundamental concept of employing indirect lighting where light is cast on to floors, walls and ceilings by concealed sources.

Computer technology is now fuelling further changes in centralizing control and allowing maximum flexibility in how lighting is used throughout the home.

Choosing lights

When planning the lighting for your house you need to think not only about the design but also the application, focus, tasks, the practical limitations of the design as well as the positioning of the controls.

Design Decide what is the most appropriate form of lighting for each room given its size and its function. If it is a narrow corridor, for instance, how do you want to light it to minimize the architectural drawbacks? What sort of ambience do you want to create?

Application Next consider the light's application. How are you going to use the room and where are the most important pieces of furniture – the dining table or the sofas and chairs in the sitting room – to be positioned? What are the floor coverings and window coverings and how much will they reflect the light back into the room?

Focus What are the main features in the room and how do you want to highlight them? This could be an architectural feature, such as a fireplace or ceiling mouldings, or it might be your own collection of pictures.

Tasks The lighting in the kitchen and bathroom are especially important. Where do you want to prepare food and how will you light the cooking area? In the bathroom you need to make sure that there is sufficient light for the area where you apply your make-up or shave. Task lighting is also important in studies and in living rooms, where you might want a reading corner.

Practical limitations When it comes to assessing the practical limitations you need to consider how easy it will be to run new wiring into the points where you require new light sources. You are likely to have to undertake a considerable degree of replastering and redecorating if you want wires to be concealed.

Controls Finally, you must decide if you want all the lights in one room controlled from a central switch by the door. How many of the lights do you want on the one circuit? How many sockets do you want – always err on the side of generosity here – and do you want to install dimmer switches, which may affect your choice of light fittings because not all are suitable for dimming? Do you need to install complete new circuits? This may be necessary in the kitchen if you are putting in a much greater range of electrical appliances than there were previously.

Types of light fitting

You can choose among three basic types of lighting: general lighting provides overall brightness in the room; task lighting gives concentrated light for special needs, such as reading or sewing; and accent lighting adds decorative highlights over, say, a picture to draw attention to special features.

The benefit of modern lighting is that you no longer have to get one light to perform several functions. In the past, table or standard lamps often had to provide both general and accent lighting. Now you can use several sources of general lighting to light the floor, walls and ceilings separately and create a different atmosphere depending on the time of day.

Above Buyers need to be able to visualize themselves in a room. Providing more than one type of lighting helps this and also creates an illusion of space. The central light floods the whole room, which is appropriate for a living room, while the under-shelf light displays the vase beneath and creates interest.

Downlighters You usually need to install several downlighters to ensure that light is spread evenly across the room, but your electrician will advise you. Low-voltage downlighters replicate the brightness of daylight, and this makes them particularly suitable for use in working areas of the house. They are also good for lighting up dark, narrow passageways.

Downlighters can be used in reception rooms, but they should not be the main source of general lighting. They should be used to emphasize one particular piece of furniture or picture. When they are used judiciously they can help make a room seem smaller and more intimate in the evening. If you install an array of downlighters in the living room, you should be able to vary the number you turn on at any one time. Too many downlighters in a room can make it over-bright and detract from the character of the room.

Most downlighters are recessed into the ceiling, so you need a certain depth in the ceiling void to accommodate them. If there is not sufficient space available or the ceiling is old and made of lath and plaster, you would probably be better opting for semi-recessed or surface-mounted lights instead.

Wall-washers These are some of the most attractive types of general lighting for living rooms. They often use florescent bulbs that are concealed behind a reflector fitting, so they are much cheaper to maintain and less trouble to install than low-voltage halogen lights. There are also wall-washers available that use ordinary and halogen bulbs.

Wall-washers are ceiling-mounted lights that cast an even glow across the wall. They contribute to a sense of breadth to a room by emphasizing the vertical walls. Depending on the colour of the wall, light will be reflected off its surface, brightening the natural light in a room. These lights work best, therefore, on pale-coloured walls. When wall-washers are used to emphasize a single wall – where pictures are displayed, for example – they will make the wall more prominent. For this reason, they are best not used in small rooms.

Uplighters These direct light upwards on to the ceiling and the glow they cast creates attractive, subdued general lighting. Uplighters can also be used to add dramatic effect to a room at night because they add height, giving an impression of a bigger space.

There is a huge choice of fittings in both style and technical design, and there are lights available for all types of bulbs. Because this type of light is not generally concealed, the style itself is more important than in the case of downlighters or wall-washers. Uplighters can be wall-mounted fittings or they can even be set in the floor, which can look particularly attractive in hallways and on staircases.

Task lighting Task lighting provides a strong local light exactly where it is needed for a specific function. In the kitchen task lights are often mounted under wall units to provide additional illumination over the cooker hob or the sink. In bathrooms they can be part of a mirror fitted over a sink to provide light for shaving and applying make-up. Although these lights can be integrated into the main lighting circuit, many task lights are stand-alone table lamps or floor-based lamps. There is a huge choice of styles, and your choice will be determined by the overall style you are creating in the house.

Accent lighting This is supplementary to the general lighting and is designed to give local illumination to features you want to highlight. A pendulum light over the dining table or a picture light are typical examples of effective accent lighting. Spotlights can also provide accent lighting, but it is important that you calculate the beam angle when you are positioning these lights. The design of spotlights reflects the fashion, so change them if they are more than 10 years old, otherwise they will obviously look out of date.

A general rule of accent lighting is that the source should be unobtrusive, keeping the focus on the object being highlighted, but sometimes the light itself becomes the ornament to be admired, as happens with dining table pendants and chandeliers, which have become fashionable again for use as central light fittings.

Flooring

To cover the floor in the bathroom and kitchen you can choose from ceramic tiles, terracotta tile linoleum, vinyl and wooden flooring. All are hard-wearing and suitable for heavy use. Tiles can, however, be cold underfoot unless you have underfloor heating. See also pages 131 and 142. For the remaining rooms of the house, carpet is the obvious choice for providing comfort and warmth, but you can also have rugs over a wood or concrete floor.

Wooden floors

The easiest way to add value to a property through flooring is to put down wooden floors in the main living rooms and hallway. These have eclipsed carpets as the covering most people prefer in these areas of hard wear. Wooden floors are more hygienic, are easier to clean and harbour fewer household mites than fitted carpets, which are thought to have contributed to the rise in asthma in the last 20 years.

Wood is also attractive in its own right, offering visual interest and texture in its graining, pattern and colour depending on the type used.

The cheapest wooden floor is the one that probably already exists, which can often be sanded down and varnished to achieve a warm, glowing surface. It is not the best choice, however, because there are usually cracks between the floorboards through which draughts and dust will come up. Many old floorboards in ordinary terraced houses were cheap pine and have warped and shrunk. They are also narrow and don't look that attractive even after your sanding efforts.

A better choice if you live in a house like this is to lay a floating wooden floor over the original surface. You can choose between laminates, which are fairly inexpensive but will last only a few years, and the more durable types, which have a layer of wood on top of a plywood base and can last for up to 40 years if they are looked after properly.

You can choose between softwoods, such as cherry and pear, or hardwoods, such as oak or iroko. For areas of heavy traffic you should always go for a hardwood finish, which will last much longer. Softwoods are prone to damage from stiletto heels and from water. Cherry is currently fashionable, but the always popular, classic choice is oak.

All woods are graded according to quality and the number of knots and graining in the wood. The finer the wood, the fewer the knots and the more expensive it will be. The flooring is usually laid in tongue-and-groove strips, but you can also buy wood-block flooring with herringbone and parquet patterns. If the floor it sits on is not level, it will not be easy to lay and the job should be left to professionals. As a rule, the more expensive the floor, the more it will cost to fit.

Carpets

In bedrooms carpet is still popular because it is soft and luxurious underfoot. Pure wool carpets are the most expensive, but for hard wear a mixture of 80 per cent wool and 20 per cent nylon is probably better. You can also buy carpets with a mixture of 50 per cent wool and 50 per cent nylon, but these often go black around the edges after only a few years.

Pure nylon carpets are a cheap solution to an immediate decorating problem, but they are shiny and unpleasant to walk on in bare feet. They do, however, have clarity of colour and a wider range of colours that cannot be produced in wool. They are also now treated to repel stains and with fire retardants.

Paints and wall coverings

The colour of the walls in the house is a personal choice, but to add maximum value to the property, you should paint the main rooms of the house in a neutral colour. Bright colours should be restricted to rooms that are not heavily used or that have a distinct function. This will help potential buyers imagine how they could live in the property, and you will put fewer people off who might not share your taste and cannot face redecorating when they move in.

Paint

The boom in DIY has led many manufacturers to improve their paints to help amateurs with home decorating, and it is now much easier to achieve a good finish with modern paint. Even so, there is still no substitute for good preparation. If you are doing up a property to get maximum value on resale you should always use professional decorators. They can achieve a much better finish than an amateur, and it really makes a difference to the overall impression of the house.

If you do decide to decorate yourself, follow a few some simple rules:

- Shop around for paint because prices vary wildly. Ask local builders where they buy their paint; they always know the cheapest source.
- When you go to buy, make sure you buy enough so that all the paint comes from a single batch, otherwise there is a risk that the second batch will not match the colour of the first.
- Prepare surfaces carefully, washing down walls and dusting before you start.
- Refill and sand any holes, or where the existing paintwork is damaged.

Paint spread over a wall always looks darker than on the chart, so it can be difficult to judge whether a colour is suitable. Buy tester pots if you are unsure – they are well worth the small investment.

For woodwork you can use either gloss or eggshell. Eggshell is currently more fashionable than gloss because the matt finish is subtler and does not show the flaws in the wood as much as gloss. Eggshell is less easy to maintain than gloss, however, as the surface is not as hard and cannot be wiped down. It ages faster, too, and white goes yellow after only a few years. You might consider gloss in areas of heavy wear, such as the kitchen where the surfaces can attract considerable grease.

Wallpapers

Wallpaper has staged a comeback in the last few years and is now fashionable again. It has the advantage of disguising flaws in the wall and can alter the perception of the size and shape of a room. It is most effective when it is used in combination with paint or other papers. In a long, narrow hall patterned wallpaper below the dado rail and plain paint above creates a greater dimension to the passageway.

When you are choosing wallpaper, always make sure that the size of the pattern matches the scale of the room. A large room can take a large pattern, but a small room should have a small pattern. But this rule can be broken if you paper just one wall and leave the rest plain.

Furnishings

The furniture in a house is always a reflection of the owner's personal taste, and it is often acquired over the years. In itself it does not usually add value to a property, because furniture usually goes with you, but in terms of presenting the house for sale, furniture is important in contributing to the overall impression of how well cared for a property is. A fine antique to set off an alcove or a finely carved bed will live in the memory of purchasers longer than the size of the room.

It is often better to remove some of your furniture when you come to sell the house, because making it less cluttered will make it look bigger. You should seek to give an impression of how people could live in your house and make it feel welcoming. See Chapter 16, pages 176–80, for more information on presenting your property to best effect.

Shelving and bookcases

Shelving and bookcases have to be excellent quality to add value to a property. Bad or inadequate shelving systems can detract from the value of a property as they can make a flat or house look shoddy. While storage space is always a plus for buyers, too many bookcases can make rooms look smaller and over cluttered.

Open shelves are best for displaying books and objects of interest, which add depth and personal touches to a room. Shelving for storage of toys, games or other essential household items is often best concealed behind cupboard doors as it is hard for them not to look untidy. Use shelving to add interest to boring, boxy rooms. Shelves under window seats or as room dividers can add valuable extra storage space in small flats.

You can use a wide variety of materials for shelving but good quality wood or glass is best. MDF can be painted and some decorative mouldings or beading will lessen its utilitarian appearance. Glass helps to reflect light around a dark room while wood will absorb reflections.

Shelves need to be adequately supported and firmly fixed to the wall. If a shelf is too thin to carry the weight placed on it, it will buckle. The traditional method is to rest the shelves on battens with brackets at each end. Additional support should be provided at intervals if shelves run along a wall – every 75cm is probably best.

Summary: Decorating

Lighting

- Nowadays, lighting is indirect and easy to manipulate according to the time of day and the atmosphere you want to create.
- The three basic types are general lighting (provides overall brightness), task lighting (concentrated light for specific needs) and accent lighting (adds decorative highlights).
- Working areas like the kitchen and study need bright, concentrated light, with softer tones in living areas.
- Planning considerations are the design of the light, its application and focus, what you want it to do, the practical limitations of the design and the position of the controls.

Flooring

- Bathroom and kitchen flooring must be hard-wearing. Ceramic and terracotta tiles, linoleum, vinyl and wood are all suitable.
- Elsewhere, carpet is the obvious choice, or rugs over wood or concrete.
- Laying a wooden floor in the main living rooms and hallway is the easiest way to add value through flooring.
- Wooden floors are hygienic, easy to clean and attractive.
- If the surface is uneven, have wooden flooring laid professionally.
- Usually, the more expensive the floor, the more it will cost to fit.

Paints and wall coverings

- To add maximum value, use a neutral colour in the main rooms and employ professional decorators, who can acheive a much better finish.
- Wallpaper is fashionable again and can disguise flaws. Ensure that the size of the pattern matches the scale of the room.

Furniture

- Although it doesn't add value, it is important in creating an overall impression.
- It can be a good idea to remove some furniture when you are trying to sell to make the house look bigger and less cluttered.

⑮ The Garden

How people would like their garden to look is usually completely at variance with the amount of work they are prepared to put in to get it to such a state. Although gardens are often described as outdoor rooms, in Britain they can be used as such for no more than about four months of the year, and spending large amounts on wooden decking or up-to-the-minute stainless steel will not add value.

Using the garden

What people want from their garden varies enormously. Some people are simply looking for a safe outside area in which children can kick a football around, others want somewhere to allow them to enjoy a satisfying hobby, still others want nothing more than a pleasant place to relax in the sun, while others are looking for a patch of ground that opens up the vistas from inside the house.

These conflicting aspirations mean that when it comes to determining how you can add value to your property through improving the garden, you are, so to speak, into difficult terrain. It is a safe bet to assume that most people prefer a garden that is not too large and that does not require too much maintenance, but perhaps the real secret of a successful garden is to create a mood and an illusion of a sanctuary where the seasons can be observed and spirits refreshed accordingly.

There is no question that outside space is a valuable commodity, which is always reflected in the price of a house. In flats especially, even the tiniest of patios or a balcony with a view will add up to 10 per cent to the asking price. When it comes to houses, where a garden is nearly always included, the added value is demonstrated by the fact that a house without a garden is always difficult to sell.

In the country, where space is less expensive, ordinary family houses with large gardens can be transformed into special properties by landscaping and planting. Here you can think about creating a series of different outdoor rooms with different functions, which can include formal areas, play areas and kitchen gardens.

Town gardens are among the most difficult to tackle. Owners may dream of landscape-designed space or Mediterranean-style arbours, but most people actually possess a long, narrow strip of grass, usually in poor condition, bordered by straggling, out-of-control shrubs and plants that manage to look miserable on even the sunniest day.

Quick transformations

If you are short of time, money, horticultural knowledge and interest there are several simple steps you can take to give an instant facelift for a season while you sell your property and that will allow you to enjoy the outside space while it is still yours.

Clearance Cut back all the hedges and shrubs and cut the grass. Clear away all rubbish, sweep up all leaves and remove the weeds, especially those on the paths. Once this is done, carry out regular maintenance to keep it tidy. This will give an immediate uplift and make the garden look bigger.

Boundaries Fences and hedges give definition to the garden plot and provide privacy from the neighbours. If the trellis is old, rotting and coming adrift from the foundation posts, replace it. Plant one or two climbers against it to soften the impact of the raw new wood. This will have the effect of softening the surrounding buildings and making your space look bigger. There are numerous plants for every aspect but take particular care with north-facing fences.

Disguises Many gardens suffer from having been paved in ugly concrete, which, over time, cracks and looks dingy and dismal. The simplest and easiest disguise is gravel, which can be made less austere by combining with some planted-up containers and, if there is suitable space, some seating.

Infuse colour Most town gardens end up only looking interesting in just one season of the year because the flowering period for most shrubs and plants is relatively short and narrow gardens do not have enough space to create interest all year round. In many gardens early summer, when spring bulbs and early-flowering shrubs are over, and late summer, when bedding plants are looking straggly and past their best, are the worst times. Add a touch of instant colour in containers. Perlagoniums are particularly useful for this, but most large stores continue to offer a range of summer bedding plants for several months and you can usually replace plants that have gone over.

Bedding plants are also the easiest way to give a lush appearance to an otherwise neglected plot. To keep a sense of coherence,

Right A simple water feature can enhance even the smallest garden. If aiming at the family market, a child-friendly example is a must as an open pond is very likely to be a deterrent to people with young children. It is worth getting even the simplest electrics in the garden installed by a professional as potential buyers will be happier that way.

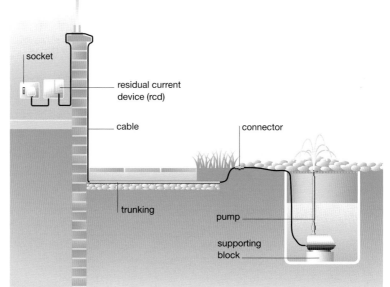

plant them in pots that are similar in style although varied in height and shape – terracotta containers are always attractive, but in a modern garden galvanized steel buckets can look sensational. Keep to similar plant types – busy lizzies or petunias, for example – to maintain an air of simple discipline. Too many different plant types can look chaotic.

Create a focal point A dramatic plant, ideally an evergreen, with an interesting texture or shape, can provide a point that will draw the eye and give coherence to a garden that otherwise lacks definition. Surround the plant with pots of seasonal flowers to enhance the interest.

Water feature Although it is now something of a cliché, the gentle sound of trickling water from a small water feature imparts a magical atmosphere and a sense of peace amid the hustle and bustle of a town. It also creates an inner focus so that the senses are diverted from other, less attractive features of the garden. You can buy simple waterspouts for mounting on a wall or an urn that bubbles up. They are run by submersible pumps and are easy to install provided you have the appropriate electric cable, which has to be run into the garden from indoors, and you must comply with building regulations.

Light Many town gardens are cast into shade, even on a bright summer's day, by overgrown trees in neighbouring gardens or high surrounding boundaries. You can, however, make your garden appear lighter simply by painting the surrounding walls and fences a pale colour. White is not necessarily the best choice for a garden, pinks and terracottas will be more sympathetic to the plants and add greater element of vibrancy.

Entertaining Most people want a garden where they can sit out on summer evenings, to entertain friends and family. You need to create an area that is dry and flat underfoot where you can put a table and chairs. Decking is the simplest material to use, and it can be laid near the house or against a wall or fence. Install a barbecue and some potted plants and you have an instant outdoor room.

Redesigning the garden

If you feel that a more serious garden transformation is required, you will have to draw up a design and make a plan. If you have only just moved into the property, take your time. You might choose to sit out the first summer while you familiarize yourself with what you already have in terms of the overall structure and the potential of the site, as well as its situation and soil type.

Assessing the plot

The first step in drawing up a new plan for any garden is to identify what cannot be changed.

Defining features Look at your plot and work out its defining features. These will include the direction in which it faces (its aspect) and therefore how much sun it will get and at what times of the day. This will help you to decide where to site any seating areas, because most people want to be able to enjoy the afternoon and evening sun. It will also define your planting

plan, as some plants need more sunlight than others. You should also note the position of walls, fences, inspection covers and large, mature trees.

Soil type Most plants grow in most types of soil, but some soils are strongly acid or alkaline, and this will determine your choice of plants. You can try to cheat nature by adding dressings to amend the soil type, but trying to change the underlying acidity or alkalinity of soil is a forlorn hope and you will only be making a great deal of work for yourself. It is better to work with what you have. Look at what is growing in the garden already and what is growing in your neighbours' gardens. Rhododendrons and camellias like acid soil; clematis and philadelphus prefer alkaline conditions. If you're still not sure, buy one of the inexpensive, easy-to-use soil-test kits from a DIY store and test the soil from several places in the garden.

Shade Shadow and where it falls are critical in determining how your garden will grow. Look at the trees you and your neighbours have that may create dry, shady areas where nothing will flourish and look out for dank corners where light never penetrates. These are problem areas and will need special attention.

Wind Although it is less of a problem in towns, wind and its prevailing direction are important factors in suburban and country gardens. Strong winds can distort and twist plants and trees, and you may have to consider planting a hedge or erecting some other barrier to reduce the damage.

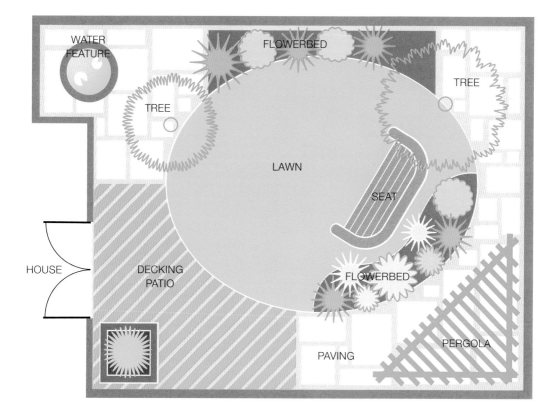

WATER FEATURE

FLOWERBED

TREE

TREE

LAWN

SEAT

HOUSE

DECKING PATIO

FLOWERBED

PAVING

PERGOLA

Above To see whether your ideas about the layout of the garden will work, it is a good idea to make a drawing. Although the broad outlines of this garden work, the water feature will be hidden and partially shaded by the smaller tree and the pergola will be in shade at lunchtime if the larger tree is too tall.

Slopes It is often best to level a steeply sloping site by creating a series of terraces, which are more useful as living spaces or for creating different planting areas.

Immediate surroundings You may want to create privacy from your neighbours as a first priority. Then, if there is an attractive feature, such as a church spire, that can be seen from the garden, your design should include that extra dimension. The 'borrowed landscape' will help to make the garden seem larger than it is, and in bigger gardens it adds a vista in which your garden is the foreground.

Preparing the design

Contemporary designs for gardens in Britain usually fall into one of two categories: the plan is either based on the idea of an outdoor room or series of rooms that serve as an extension of the house, or it is based on the notion of the country tamed and brought to town. The outdoor room is dominated by the formal elements of the design, while the country garden seeks to dissolve boundaries and relies on loose and informal planting. Some gardens incorporate elements of both, but to be successful, one theme must predominate.

The outdoor room In an outdoor room the boundaries are clearly defined and are a feature of the garden, as is the floor, which is usually covered in paving. You rarely find lawn or grass used in this type of garden. Planting is often in containers or raised beds, and the aim is to provide a decorative but low-maintenance area. There can be much use of fairly simple plants, such as box for hedging, and pattern and symmetry are used to create a planned, harmonious atmosphere. The central focus in such a garden in a town will be the eating area. This type of garden is currently much in fashion, reflecting the trends in interior design. While formal scheming is suitable for small gardens, in a large garden it can become boring unless the garden is broken up into different segments and there is some variety to stimulate the eye.

The design of this type of garden depends on geometry, and getting the proportions right is critical to its visual success. The size of the paving stones is often the key on which all other proportions in the garden are based. If you want

Above A small area of decking can provide a cosmetic fix for an untidy area of paving. A simple patio reached from the living room or kitchen gives the feeling of an 'outdoor room', making the house seem larger. Simple wooden furniture works well with decking and is more sophisticated than plastic.

Builder's rubble

Many new houses have gardens that are nothing more than a couple of inches of topsoil scattered over heaps of builder's rubble. If you have the time and energy it is worth getting rid of the rubble, which often contains cement and concrete, and buying in some decent topsoil. At least then, when you do get round to planting anything in the garden, it will have a half-decent chance of growing. If you don't want to go to the expense of getting rid of the rubble, use it in raised beds or as the basis of a scree or gravel garden.

to make the garden look longer, you should lay the paving in vertical lines. A mix of horizontal and vertical lines will break up the space.

The country garden The country garden is more romantic in feeling. Planting climbers and wall shrubs will conceal the boundaries and break up the garden into separate components. The use of hard materials is scaled down, and there will usually be a lawn, which allows children to play more easily, so this garden is often found with family houses. The disadvantage of this type of garden is that it can become overgrown and out of control within only a few years. Most people make the mistake of overplanting or of including plants that are so vigorous and thuggish that they take over the garden completely.

Rules of design

Observe a few basic rules when you are designing a garden.

Simplicity Keep the broad lines of the design as simple as possible. Overcomplicated schemes tend to make a garden look smaller and the work of an amateur.

Variety If you are dividing the garden into separate rooms, do not make them equal in size because this makes it difficult to decide on the purpose of the garden. If one-third of the outside area is a seating space and the remainder is planted, this will show that the garden is a peaceful, restful place. If your seating area takes up two-thirds of the space, your garden is better suited to relaxing and alfresco entertaining on summer evenings.

Curves A path linking the various sections of a garden forms the spine of the design. Although curved paths will soften the overall effect and prevent the garden from looking too boxy, a path that curves for no reason looks fussy, especially in a small garden. A straight or gently curved path that takes the eye down the longest dimension of a small garden by crossing the diagonal can create a satisfying illusion of greater space.

Size In addition to choosing plants that will tolerate the soil type in your garden, make sure that you do not plant anything that will grow so large it quickly becomes out of scale with the garden as a whole and with your house. One or two tall plants or even a tree (depending on the size of your garden and the species of tree) will give the necessary height against which smaller plants can be offset and carry the eye upwards. However, remember that plants grow, and you must take care that you do not plant anything that in five years' time will be robbing you of light in either the garden or the house.

Illusions To create an illusion of space, design your garden so that not all of it is visible at first glance. Having areas that have to be 'discovered' will help to create a sense of mystery. Emphasizing the longest dimension can often make a garden appear larger than it actually is, so choose plants that will direct the eye down its length.

False perspective Create a false perspective by using internal screens, such as a hedge, arch or trellis. It may mean sacrificing the last few feet of the garden, but you can use the screen to disguise a tool shed or the compost heap.

The garden floor

The choice of a surfacing material and its relationship with the green areas of a garden are among the most important decisions in any redesign, and in a small garden, the garden floor will be the main visual focus of the entire design. For most gardens a good balance is to have no more than three changes of surface.

Soft surfaces

In a family garden a safe play area for children will be a priority, so if this is the group you have identified as your target market, make sure you have a lawn or suitable space for children.

Above Gardens in the country do not just have to remain self-contained: they can 'borrow' from the surrounding landscape. One way of emphasizing a particularly good view or feature is to frame it with an arch or boundary plants.

Grass The cheapest surface is turf. It has much to recommend it, as it is durable, tough and good if there are children, who are less likely to hurt themselves if they fall on grass than on a hard surface. The disadvantage is the maintenance. Grass has to be cut regularly during the growing period, which now lasts well into autumn, and if it is to look really good you need to rake, weed, feed and scarify it, not to mention trimming the edges. If the area that should be lawn is filled with weeds and rather rank, broad-leaved grasses, consider digging it up and starting again. You can either sow seed, which will take a season, or lay turves, which will give you instant lawn. For best results the new lawn should be on a level, weed-free, well-drained site, or you will simply find that you have replaced one unattractive lawn with another.

Large lawns always look better than small, bitty ones. In many town gardens the small lawn is also the path to other parts of the garden, so it suffers from too much wear and tear and too little light and air. It will not flourish and you should consider an alternative.

Bark chippings If your garden is so small that a lawn is going to be more trouble than it is worth, consider clearing and levelling the area and covering it with a permeable membrane over which you can put a thick layer of bark chippings. This provides a soft surface for a children's play area, and apart from raking the surface and topping up the chippings from time to time, it is much less work than a lawn because the membrane stops weeds from growing up, and any that germinate in the chippings can be quickly and easily removed.

Hard surfaces

Even if you have a lawn, there will be areas of the garden, such as paths and patios, that will require hard surfacing. There is a considerable choice of materials, ranging from wooden decking to brick, stone, concrete and even terracotta tiles, which can extend from the house to give a feeling of continuity and expand the space both inside and out.

Hard surfaces are low maintenance and are the obvious choice in gardens that are deficient in sunlight. They can be slippery in wet weather, however, and a huge expanse of the same material is hard on the eye and makes a garden look flat and boring. You need to break it up with beds and borders to create variety and pockets of interest.

Concrete slabs are the cheapest material on the market but are dull in colour, flat in texture, monotonous on the eye and have an unfriendly feel. Many designs are imitations of more natural stones, but they tend to look like imitations. Concrete is being used in more exciting ways in modernist gardens, and this has brought the material back into fashion. It isn't ideal choice for grey English light, however, and to look its best it needs bright sunlight and lots of greenery to bring out its more attractive qualities.

Sandstone A more interesting choice than concrete, sandstone can be the ideal material. It is durable and has attractively mellow, subtly varied tones. It complements other materials, such as bricks and wood, so will blend well whether used in town or country gardens. Although it is much more expensive than

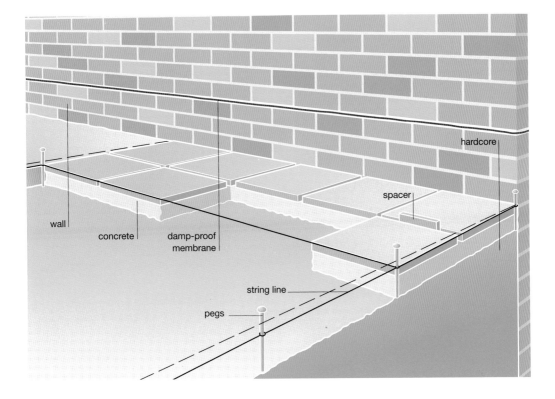

wall | concrete | damp-proof membrane | hardcore | spacer | string line | pegs

concrete, it is worth the extra money if you can afford it. There is considerable choice available, so shop around.

York stone Perhaps the best stone of all is old York stone, of which plentiful supplies could be found 20–30 years ago when the old textile mills closed down, but it is now in short supply. Expect to pay about £1,000 a metre (yard), so this is probably only worth doing in expensive properties or where you plan to stay for a long time. You can obtain new York stone, and although this is more severe in tone than the old variety, it blends well with gravel. This is an ideal material for paths.

Above When making improvements to any home, it is worth spending time and attention on getting things right. This is particularly important with structural work. When laying a patio, there should always be at least two bricks between the damp-proof membrane and the top of the slabs, and the patio should slope away from the house by 16mm per metre (⅝in per yard).

Limestone The vogue for limestone in the house has spread into the garden. Architects who are keen to dissolve the boundaries between the house and garden will lay limestone in the kitchen and extend it into the garden. It looks good when it is first laid, but over a period of years this is unlikely to be a happy choice. The pale stone will discolour with pollution and as algae and lichen grow. It is also prone to frost damage, which will quickly make the surface pitted and uneven.

Slate has become a popular choice for minimalist and modern gardens. It is a hard-wearing material but never looks quite right in a domestic setting. Its use is probably best limited to accenting water features or other focal points. It is also expensive, and tends to split in frost.

Granite setts are an ideal choice for areas such as paths and driveways that have to withstand heavy traffic. The setts are small pieces of stone, which can be laid in intricate patterns, and they are usually set in a bed of sand and cement. The surface is uneven, providing a safe, nonslip surface, but this makes them unsuitable for patios or seating areas. They look particularly attractive when mixed with other paving stones or bricks. Setts are not cheap but will last for years. Concrete setts are cheaper but do not look as attractive as granite.

Bricks can look wonderful on garden paths, especially when their colour harmonizes with the bricks used for the house. Make sure that you use water-resistant bricks for your paths and patios, otherwise they will be damaged by frost.

Much of the interest in brick paths comes from the ways in which the bricks are laid out. They are suitable for use in curved paths and to form intricate patterns. Narrow bricks laid in a herringbone pattern are often seen in the finest period English gardens. Patterns blend particularly well with a formal planting scheme, such as a herb garden or an Elizabethan knot garden. Laying bricks lengthways will indicate direction; laying them crossways will make the path look wider.

Bricks paths require regular maintenance, otherwise they become covered with moss and lichen, which makes them slippery and dangerous when they are wet. A high-pressure jet of water will usually clear the surface quickly, but a scrubbing brush and horticultural disinfectant works just as well.

Prices for bricks will vary depending on quality.

Gravel is the ideal material for small front gardens, paths and small areas of larger gardens, such as around a focal point. It is comparatively inexpensive to buy and lay, and provides an instant surface. Muted shades of beige and grey tend to look better than bright white or even the coloured chippings that are increasingly available. One disadvantage of gravel is that the stones travel, so if you lay it on a path, make sure that the edges are raised slightly – on-edge bricks or strips of wood, for example, will prevent the gravel from escaping on to the lawn.

Tiles Tiles are particularly suitable for a patio and barbecue area, where it is important to keep the floor clean. They also look wonderful.

You need to make sure that the tiles you choose are suitable for outdoor use because many are not frost-resistant. You can use ceramic tiles, terrazzo tiles and some of the natural Italian stone tiles, but this is not a cheap option.

Decking This American import has enjoyed enormous popularity in the last 15 years. A well-laid deck of good-quality timber does look attractive with plants, and it is comparatively inexpensive and relatively easy to lay. It is also a good choice for a patio or dining area that slopes, since the decking can easily be raised above the ground to provide a level surface. The disadvantages are that the wood can rot after only a few years and that, in the British climate, the surfaces get wet and slimy, making them dangerous and unappealing. Decking is

Above Bricks are pleasing to look at in small areas such as patios. Try to use paving bricks that are the same as the house bricks to add to the idea of an outside room. Vary the layout to create optical illusions of length or width.

Above Timber decking is excellent for enclosed courtyard town gardens where it is difficult to cultivate a healthy grass lawn. Easy maintenance is an added bonus.

best confined to small areas near the house, to a roof terrace or balcony or to a sunny spot away from the house.

Boundaries

A property's boundaries are decisive in establishing the character of the garden and are essential components of a redesign to add value. Make it a priority to replace cheap chain-link or wire-mesh fencing, which does not provide any privacy and lacks charm. Brick walls topped with wooden trellis are probably the ideal choice for a town garden so that you can grow plants to soften the boundary and enhance privacy.

Timber fencing is also attractive and serves as a useful windbreak without restricting the circulation of air in a garden. It does have a limited life of 10–15 years, because the wooden posts that support it tend to rot.

New walls and fences should not be higher than 2m (6ft 6in), and you may need planning permission for a new fence along a front boundary, so check with your local authority. Make sure that the footings for any new fence posts do not trespass over the boundary between your and your neighbour's property.

Hedges are an attractive and effective screen, especially in country gardens, but they take years to establish and need regular maintenance and trimming. They are often used in front gardens in towns to give a house greater privacy from the street, but they are not an ideal choice. When mature they will take light from the ground floor and basement of the house. They also are used by passers-by as a convenient place to put rubbish.

The other disadvantages of hedges are that they can become woody at the bottom and grow too tall for the garden. They are hungry for nutrients, taking goodness from the soil, and leave an area of dry shade where it is difficult for anything else to grow. Hedges are, however, the best choice for rural gardens where they blend well with the surrounding area.

Roof terraces

If you are buying a flat where there is potential to install a roof terrace you will be able to add thousands to the value of the property. Outside space in any flat is a huge bonus in itself, but a roof terrace is best of all. Upper-floor flats are always popular with buyers because of the extra light and the greater security of being above ground, and if you can introduce somewhere to sit out on summer evenings, your flat will have everything the buyer might reasonably want.

The usual place to install a roof terrace is on the flat roof of an extension. If you are building a mansard-roof loft extension, you can create space for a terrace outside the window. You will need to get planning permission, which isn't always easy because neighbours often object to the loss of privacy and being overlooked. It is easier if you own two storeys of the building or if you own the flat roof of the extension.

The critical structural factor is the weight that the roof will have to bear. Large containers and raised beds filled with moist soil weigh a tremendous amount, and if the roof is not properly strengthened, this could be an extremely dangerous project. The district surveyor will keep a keen eye on your progress to see that building regulations are met.

The other problem with gardening on a roof terrace is wind. Because you are higher up, you and your plants are more exposed to the prevailing wind and being caught in eddies caused by surrounding buildings. You will have to erect screens to protect your plants, or your choice will be extremely limited. Wooden screens or even glass bricks can be used. Whichever material you choose, it must be firmly anchored and you will have to accept that the view may be restricted.

Watering plants on a roof terrace can also turn into something of a chore. The best option is to run a waterpipe out on to the terrace so that you can have a tap. If that is not possible try to make sure that you are near to a water supply in the house, whether the kitchen or bathroom. You don't want to have to carry watering cans up three flights of stairs.

Swimming pools

Swimming pools are a slippery issue. Some agents advise against them because they use up space in the garden that might look more attractive with plants and trees. This particularly applies where space is at a premium, such as in cities. Out of town, pools are more popular, especially with families with children who regard them as useful places for entertaining friends during school holidays.

The style of the pool should be in keeping with the property. Done well, it can be the decisive factor for even the most indecisive buyers. The cheapest option is an outdoor pool, which can either be made of concrete or plastic liner. You can expect to pay around £30,000 for a decently sized concrete pool. Plastic liners are cheaper, but even so you are unlikely to get one for much less than £15,000. Indoor pools are more expensive, the cost escalating with the amount of construction work required, and you could easily spend upwards of £50,000. For the ultimate in luxury, spa pools are now available in domestic settings.

Installing a swimming pool is specialized work and requires some technical expertise. SPATA is the trade association for the swimming pool industry in the UK. It supplies an information pack, which includes a contract checklist of useful questions to ask anyone tendering for the work.

Even using the experts will not save you from headaches during the construction phase. You should make sure that the person you appoint to supervise the work has the time to do so. In other words: do not leave this to the pool designers, who will be too busy working on design projects. The other risk is that much of the equipment used in pools, steam rooms and spas is highly specialist and even the designers are unfamiliar with some of it.

There are a number of disadvantages to swimming pools. They need to be maintained, cleaned and kept filled with clean, sparkling water. If you choose to contract this out, the maintenance charges are expensive. If you don't have a regular contract with a maintenance firm, you could find that if something goes wrong the pool is out of action for months while you wait for a spare part to be supplied and fitted. If you have young children you will have to consider putting up some fencing to prevent them straying into the pool unattended.

It is worth installing a pool only if you want one. They do not add value to the property except in the most expensive houses, where they are probably now regarded as an essential extra.

Tennis courts

For buyers of country houses a tennis court is one of the most popular extras in the garden. It is a sport that can be enjoyed by people of all ages, and the number of private courts is on the increase. Families like them because they can be used not just for tennis but for riding bicycles and playing ball games. They are more popular than swimming pools because they are cheaper and easier to maintain and can be used more often. Children need less supervision when they are playing tennis than they do in a pool, and so it is easier to make it the centre of their social life in the summer with parties and barbecues to accompany the matches.

A court with a hard surface will cost between £20,000 and £30,000 to install and add about the same in value to the house. You do need at least half an acre of grounds to put one in.

Hard surfaces are more popular than grass courts because of the greater ease of maintenance. Apart from having to be mown, grass can become slippery in wet weather, and moles leave the surface uneven. Grass courts are, however, cheaper to lay than hard courts – it will cost about £15,000 to level the ground and lay the turf. There are different types of hard surfaces to choose from, some more expensive than others. The most expensive cushioned courts will cost around £50,000. If you are installing a court for the first time don't forget to include the cost of levelling the ground.

Tennis courts do need planning permission, and councils are reluctant to grant it if the court is being placed in an adjoining field rather than in the garden itself because they don't want leisure facilities to encroach on the countryside. However, permission is not needed for a court within the garden, but don't forget that you will need permission for the fencing if it is more than 2m (6ft 6in) high. Neighbours can object if the tennis court turns their view into an eyesore. And do be sensitive about the lighting you install for evening play – bright floodlights will irritate people who like their evening gardens to remain dark.

If there is space, try to site the court out of the immediate sight line of the house because they are not that beautiful to look at and stray balls crossing the patio will be dangerous. If too much of the garden is taken up by the court, you run the risk of devaluing your property.

Summary: The Garden

- Outside space is valuable: in flats it can add 10 per cent, while houses without gardens are difficult to sell.
- What people want from their garden varies enormously and such conflicting aspirations make it difficult to determine what adds value, although most people don't want too much maintenance.

Quick transformations
- **Clearance:** cutting back hedges and shrubs, clearing leaves and weeds, and mowing the grass will make the garden seem bigger.
- **Boundaries:** replace rotting trellis and fencing, and soften with plants.
- Disguise ugly features where possible.
- Add instant colour using plants in containers.
- Focal points, water features and outdoor seating areas make a garden more attractive.

Redesigning the garden
- Identify first what you cannot change: aspect, soil type, shade, wind, slopes and immediate surroundings.
- Choice of surfacing materials is crucial. Generally, avoid having more than three changes of surface. Hard surfaces are low-maintenance and good where there isn't much sun, but too much of one type can make the garden look boring.
- Boundaries are decisive in establishing the character of the garden. To add value, replace cheap chain-link or wire-mesh fencing.
- Potential to install a roof terrace can add thousands to the value of a flat.
- Swimming pools are costly and high maintenance; They do not add value, except in the most expensive houses.

Part 4
Realizing a Profit

16 Selling your House

It doesn't matter how good the quality of the building work has been on the roof nor how much you have spent on the computer-controlled sound system, to get the best price for your property it must be well presented. At its simplest, this means the property should look like a home into which people can imagine themselves moving with minimum effort and maximum pleasure.

Presentation

Television makeover programmes leave you with the impression that good presentation involves the outlay of several hundred if not thousands of pounds. While this may be necessary in neglected properties, in many cases, it is more a matter of looking at your home with fresh eyes – as if you had never seen it before – and sorting the problems that you have long ceased to notice any more.

If in doubt, ask a friend to give you a candid appraisal of what might put him or her off if he or she were viewing the house as a prospective buyer.

The two most important aspects of presentation, which are also the most straightforward and obvious, are that the house is clean and tidy. You must also consider how light and airy the house appears and whether the potential purchasers will be able to imagine themselves living in your space.

Cleaning

Before your house goes on the market you must clean it thoroughly. This is the single most

Checklist for cleaning

Kitchen

- Thoroughly clean work surfaces and appliances outside and in (including the oven) to remove all traces of grease.
- Clean the fridge and defrost the freezer.
- Clear out the kitchen cupboards, throwing out old tins, herbs and spices and anything that has had time to accumulate dust.
- Wash the floor scrupulously.
- Buy a new waste bin if necessary, preferably a stainless steel one, which is less prone to staining.

Bathroom

- Clean the bath, basin, and toilet and use limescale remover to get rid of any signs of hard water.
- Clean the taps until they sparkle.
- Wash tiles and remove all watermarks.
- Clean any mirrors.
- Pay particular attention to the grouting around the shower and bath, which can turn black with mould over time – there are special cleaners to remove this but bleach and an old nailbrush work wonders.

General

- Get the windows cleaned, outside and in.
- Wipe down skirting boards to remove dust.
- Clean fingermarks off paintwork with a cream cleaner.
- Dust all surfaces, especially windowsills.
- Vacuum the carpets and wash the hard floor surfaces.
- Use upholstery shampoo on sofas and chairs to remove stains.
- Replace defective light bulbs.
- Clean paint and other signs of dirt from sockets and light switches.
- Dust bookshelves and lightly vacuum books, which are dust traps.
- Tidy the garden, weeding thoroughly and removing accumulated old rubbish – you might have to get in a gardener for the day to help you.
- Clear out the loft, cellar and garage and any other large storage cupboards so that they don't overflow when they are opened for inspection.

important piece of preparation you can do. Bring in the professionals if you do not have the time to do it properly yourself. Otherwise, use the checklist above of essential jobs to help you. Remember to keep cleaning it regularly while the property is on the market.

Tidying

Once the house is clean, the next step is decluttering. Most of us have far too many possessions, which we accumulate with little thought, and now is as good a time as any to get rid of some of them. You will have to do it anyway when you move, so you might as well start early. This is particularly important if you are moving house because your family has grown and you are bursting at the seams. It is essential that you avoid giving the impression to buyers that the house is too small, so if necessary, hire some storage or rent a garage in which you can store surplus furniture and belongings while you sell.

Books and magazines are some of the worst offenders when it comes to clutter. Overcrowded bookshelves piled up with cheap holiday paperbacks and piles of old magazines instantly make a house look untidy, too small and rather depressing. Throw away or give to charity what you are not likely to read again and put the rest into storage.

In the kitchen clear the work surfaces and put away all the equipment, with the possible exceptions of the kettle and toaster. Expensive bottles of olive oil, a bowl of fresh fruit and a small wine rack (filled with bottles) can be on display. In the bathroom pare down the make-up and bath oils to the minimum. Put the cleaning materials out of sight.

In the living areas put all the toys out of sight in cupboards. Take out oversized pieces of furniture and keep the atmosphere simple. Decoration in reception rooms is critical.

Keep the bedrooms tidy, especially the children's rooms, and make sure the bed linen looks clean and fresh. Use plain bed linen in simple colours. Patterned linen might be too masculine or too feminine for some people's taste.

All this takes some discipline, and it has to be maintained while the house is on the market. Look at the checklist above to make sure that

> ## Checklist for tidying
>
> - Put dirty clothes out of sight.
> - Do the ironing regularly and don't leave piles of washing lying around.
> - Hide the vacuum cleaner and ironing board.
> - Don't leave clothes out to dry indoors.
> - Do the washing up after every meal and keep the kitchen tidy and spotless (see cleaning checklist, page 177).
> - Keep the bathroom gleaming (see cleaning checklist, page 177).
> - Empty bins and put rubbish outside.
> - Keep the desk and study clear of papers.
> - Make the beds properly every morning.
> - Keep the house smelling fresh.
> - If necessary, empty ashtrays several times a day.
> - Air the house regularly.
> - Fill the garden with seasonal bedding plants or bulbs to provide instant colour.

you maintain the high standards while your property is up for sale. It will be worth the effort, although you might have to make extra time for the tasks.

Adding light

Top of many people's list of priorities when they are buying a property is that the house should be light. There are a number of tricks that interior designers use to compensate for rooms where there is a limited amount of natural light.

The use of mirrors is the best way to enhance limited light. They are attractive in themselves and they can reflect light from the window back into the room. Simple measures to help show the property at its best include drawing the curtains right back and keeping internal doors open to filter light through the property. If you have a double reception room with windows at both ends, this is the time to leave the interconnecting doors wide open – double-aspect rooms are much more attractive than rooms with windows on just one wall. If a room is decorated in a dark colour you should consider repainting it white, which will make it look bigger immediately.

For evening viewings you should illuminate the rooms with side lamps rather than overhead lighting. The exceptions to this rule are the kitchen and bathroom, both of which should be brightly lit. Optional extras would be to use soft glow bulbs and to light candles and fires, if appropriate, to create a welcoming feeling and sense of atmosphere.

Defining function

Every prospective buyer will have different ideas of how the house could be used according to their own needs, but it is nonetheless important that every room in the house is seen to have a well-defined function.

Adding the 'wow' factor

Minor details can transform an ordinary property into something special. Invest in a few healthy plants, fluffy towels and crisp bed linen to give the impression of a loved and cared-for home. Look at magazines for inspiration and some

Example

If you have a two-bedroom house and one bedroom is used as a study, you might consider moving your desk and computer elsewhere for the period of sale so that you can show the second bedroom in its rightful function.

Similarly, if you use the dining room as a space for the children to do their homework while you all eat in the kitchen, you should present it formally as a dining room when you are selling the house. It will look neater, and buyers will like the idea that there is a place for entertaining guests without them seeing the inner workings of the kitchen while a meal is prepared.

ideas of the latest fashion in home accessories. High-street shops will provide these final touches for little cost.

Flowers Simplicity is always appealing, and the fresh flowers that are so popular with house doctors are perfect for reception rooms. Choose flowers that will provide an accent of colour. Fragrance is a matter of taste, but lilies can be overpowering towards the end of their life, so are probably best avoided. Freesias, on the other hand, have a delicate scent that fills the whole house and are always delightful. Daffodils and tulips are cheap and are a promise of brighter days ahead if you are showing your property in winter.

Art If you really want to make a statement about your house, you should think about the pictures on your walls. Art sells a house like nothing else, but there is an important caveat: it has to be the right art for your prospective market. During the 1980s 19th-century watercolours, hunting scenes and oil paintings of remote ancestors were fine – they may still be fine in a country house – but they will not work in a cutting-edge loft conversion.

All buyers have aspirations for the property they are going to spend so much money on, and one or two well-chosen pictures can help them to fall in love with your home.

Appointing an agent

Once you have the house in a state where you think it is ready to go on the market, your next step is to get it valued. Estate agents provide valuations and at the same time, in the hope of being appointed to sell it for you, much good advice for free. It is a good idea to get several estate agents to value your property – three is probably the ideal number to approach. You will find that their suggestions will vary and often by wide margins, and you should always ask why they have arrived at the price they suggest.

Do not necessarily appoint the agent who gives you the highest valuation. Agents often overvalue in order to secure your business, and then the property goes on the market at the suggested price only to struggle to secure serious interest. After six weeks the agent will tell you that it is overpriced and to achieve a sale, the price must be reduced. By this stage you will have wasted nearly two months, and your property is now being marketed as

reduced in price, looking less appealing than when it was new on the market. On the other hand, the advantage of trying a high price is that in a strong market you might just get it, and if you don't try, you will never know. You will need to be flexible in your approach to try this tactic.

Apart from the suggested sale price, you need to establish with the agent at your first meeting how much commission they will charge you and their detailed suggestions for marketing your house. A good agent will usually have a pretty good idea of the likely buyers for the property and the best ways of reaching them.

Ask the agent how many similar properties to yours they have sold recently and what their experience was with those. It is no use appointing an agent specializing in grand country house sales to market your little flat in the village high street. Your potential buyers will be looking in more modest agents' windows.

How do they go about selling?

You need to know what kind of property details they will prepare, how they use the Internet for marketing and whether they propose to advertise in newspapers and magazines. Ask if they feel there is anything you can do to improve presentation. If they propose a high price, ask them how long they give it until they suggest a reduction and how they would relaunch a property at a reduced price.

You also want to get some idea of the service the agent provides to you while the property is being marketed. Initially, the agent will contact everyone on their register who has expressed an interest in your type of property, so there should be an early flurry of viewings.

Ideally, you should expect to hear from the agent once a week with details of how many have seen the property and the feedback from those viewings. If the property is well presented and there are no obvious disadvantages but no offers have come in after three or four weeks, it is time for a serious discussion about what is happening. It may be that the market has softened and you should consider a price reduction. Are the right buyers being targeted? Is the agent pushing hard enough to get decisions out of buyers?

What role will they play once an offer is accepted?

Marketing the property is only half the battle in selling your house. The other critical question you need to ask is how the agent will handle the process from offer to exchange of contract. You need to be assured that a senior negotiator will always be available to help you when the going gets rough. A good agent will know who they can call on in local solicitors' offices and the local authority in case searches get delayed in bureaucracy. Because you may have to depend heavily on the agent at critical points in the sale, it is important that you like and communicate well with the person you appoint, and that you feel you can trust them.

When you appoint the agent, you will be asked to sign a contract. Take care to read the small print. In particular, check to see how long you will be tied to them. Many sellers become frustrated with their agents if there are no offers after a period and may want to change agents. The contract should allow you to do this without detriment to yourself.

Terms of agency agreements

Be aware of the different types of agreement you can have with an estate agent.

Sole agent You appoint one agent to handle the sale exclusively, and in return the commission rate is lower than under other agreements. Make sure that the agent's offices are well located because they must be on the buyers' lists of target agencies when they are looking. You can still sell privately even if you have appointed an agent, but you cannot sell to anyone introduced to you by the agent.

Joint sole agents This is where you appoint two agents and the commission is split between them. It can be a useful tactic if your property lies between two centres and would be of interest to buyers in both.

Multiple agency This is where you appoint several agents to handle the sale. Although this achieves a wider coverage than sole agency, it is not always the best route. Buyers will always look in most of the local agencies at least once, and if the same property comes up several times, you might give the impression that you are desperate to sell. There might also be variations in price and details. The commission rates are also higher to reflect that the commission will be split among several agents.

Viewings

Many agents now routinely do accompanied viewings on all their properties, and you will not necessarily have to show prospective buyers round yourself. If the agent does offer this service, it is well worth paying for, even if the commission rates are higher to reflect their additional time. Not least, it is vital security, especially for people who live on their own and for whom it is inherently risky to show a stranger round their house by themselves.

Estate agents are trained to sell. By the time they bring viewers round, they should have some knowledge of their circumstances and what they need. The agent will be able to point out where your house meets their objectives and explain away any defects they might spot. As it is not the agent's own home, they will not be personally offended by any of the comments made by the viewer and will listen to any criticisms more objectively than you, the seller, can.

If you do find yourself at home when buyers come to view, it is a good idea to stay in the background unless they specifically want to ask you questions. Give them time to view and allow them space. It is important not to appear desperate. Make sure that the temperature in the house is comfortable when you are in.

Selling in a hurry

Selling a house can often involve a battle of psychological wits. There are some sensible precautions you should take and have in mind even as you call the first agent for a valuation.

The first is that you should try to make sure that all building work is finished. If you have left the bathroom untiled or the kitchen without some vital appliances, it will look as if you have run out of money and cannot afford to finish the work. Buyers will immediately be tempted to knock a chunk off the price they are prepared to offer for the property.

Next, be careful about how much of your personal circumstances and your reasons for moving you disclose to the agents, let alone prospective buyers. Discretion is sensible simply from the point of view of your own security, but if you are selling because you are short of cash, you don't really want anyone else to know because they will assume you are a forced seller and reduce their offer accordingly. If you have been made redundant, talk of relocation; if you have to move somewhere smaller, talk about no longer needing the space because the children have left home or an ageing parent has died. Talk of moving to Spain for the sun or to the country to bring up the children or to be closer to ageing parents. Give any reason other than financial distress.

If you are selling because you are going through a divorce, keep the marital discord out of sight of the agent and buyers. Agree with your partner that you will put the property up for sale before you speak to the agents. Once an agent has an inkling that there might be problems getting a property sale to exchange of contract because of disputes between the joint owners, they will tread warily in marketing the property and in how far they will be prepared to push buyers on your behalf.

If you are seriously short of money because you are struggling to keep up the mortgage payments, try to ensure that you sell the house yourself rather than leaving it to the bank or building society. Tell your mortgage provider about your situation and agree a strategy with them for the disposal of the property to delay a foreclosure. If you bury your head in the sand and hope that your problems will go away, you may face the humiliation of having the sale forced by the bank or building society, and they will be much less interested in the sale than you are. Indeed, you might find that your property has been put up for auction as a repossession, when it will probably raise enough to repay the debt but could well leave you with no profit.

Receiving an offer

At last – the agent rings you with news that someone has made an offer on the property. The bad news is that it is 10 per cent below the asking price. Do you accept it? The questions you ask the agent here are critical. You should expect the agent to have had a detailed conversation with the buyers about their circumstances. Do they have anything to sell? Will you be in a chain? Does the agent think he can push the buyer into an improved offer if you turn this down?

On their part, the agent will be looking to see how flexible and willing you are to do a deal. The agent's interest is in getting the house under offer, and although they want to get the best price possible, they have to push both sides to a compromise. You and the agent should both know enough about what other houses have sold for locally to judge whether this offer is worth considering.

If you decide to turn this offer down, the agent will probably ask you at what price you would be prepared to settle. This is so that when they go back to the buyer, they can give an indication of where a second, more realistic offer should be pitched. Another tactic is to suggest splitting the difference between what the buyer has offered and what you want.

There are other tactics for getting a higher price. You could, for example, include fixtures and fittings that you might otherwise have taken away. Curtains, carpets and removable electric appliances, such as the washing machine, are all negotiable.

Conditions on the timing of exchange and completion of contracts should also be covered at this point. It is worth coming down in price if the buyer offers a four- to six-week exchange of contract. In a seller's market, you can insist on this as a condition of the sale price.

The experience of the agent is critical at this stage of the sale. So if you have any concerns that the agent handling the deal is too junior, ask to speak to the manager before you commit yourself to any agreement. In England and Wales all offers are subject to contract and nothing is binding at this stage (house purchase in Scotland is different, see page 47).

Once the property is under offer, your solicitor will handle most of the work ahead of exchange of contract. Completion must follow within 28 days of exchange unless there is an agreement to delay the date.

When to take the property off the market

Once you have accepted an offer, you do not have to take your property off the market immediately. For example, if the only offer you have to date is 10 per cent lower than the asking price, or if it comes from a buyer who is unable to move as quickly as you, you can accept the offer but still continue to show the property until you are satisfied that you have secured the best possible deal.

In such instances, the potential buyer might ask you to take the property off the market while they try either to raise more money or to speed up the sale of their own property. If you agree to such a proposal, it is wise to set a time limit of, say, four weeks.

Selling privately

Selling privately is always tempting at the outset when you calculate just how much you are going to have to pay the estate agent and think about all the better things you could do with that sum of money.

If you decide to do it yourself you will still have some costs, because you will have to pay for the marketing and advertising of the property. The best place to advertise is in a local property magazine for sales of up to £250,000. For more expensive properties consider newspapers and the specialist websites for private sales, which will generate the most interest (see Useful Addresses, pages 193–200). Look at the way other advertisements are written to get an idea of what you should include.

Before you place an advertisement you need to prepare your own details on the property and take the room measurements. You also need to take some photographs to post on the website or to make available to prospective viewers. More importantly, you will have to make the time available to conduct all the viewings yourself, including the many no-shows. You will also have to handle all the negotiations when it comes to receiving an offer.

The biggest disadvantage of selling privately, however, is that buyers expect to get properties slightly cheaper than they would have to pay through an agent. They know you are saving the fees and want some, if not all, of those benefits themselves. An agent can justify your asking price much more easily than you can because they have facts and figures on similar properties at their fingertips. Moreover, agents are more adept at handling negotiations than you because they are not emotionally involved and can defuse tensions effectively. However, if you are not put off by any of this, selling privately saves a great deal of money.

Summary: Selling your House

To get the best price, your property must be well presented. See page 177 for a cleaning checklist.

- Tidy up and declutter. If necessary, hire storage space for surplus belongings while you sell.
- Clear kitchen work surfaces and in the bathroom, keep toiletries to a minimum and cleaning materials out of sight.
- Keep the property clean and tidy while it is on the market.
- Make the house feel as light as possible.

Appointing an agent

- Get several estate agents to value your property.
- Establish the sale price, their commission and detailed suggestions for marketing.
- You must like and trust the person you appoint.
- Agents appointed can be sole agent, joint sole agent or multiple agency.
- Read the small print of any contract that you sign.
- It is worth paying extra for the agent to do the viewings.

Selling in a hurry

- Make sure all building work is finished.
- Never give financial distress as a reason for selling.
- Keep marital discord out of sight.
- If you are struggling with mortgage payments, endeavour to sell yourself, rather than leaving it to the bank or building society.

Receiving an offer

- If the offer is too low, find out about the buyer's circumstances. Consider negotiating on fixtures and fittings, splitting the difference with the buyers and holding them to a quick sale.
- You can keep the property on the market until you satisfy yourself that the offer you have is the best you're likely to get.

Selling privately

- Although it can save a lot of money, you will have to do the marketing and advertising, prepare the details, conduct all the viewings and undertake all the negotiation.
- Many prospective buyers expect a discount.

⑰ Letting a Property

In the years when house prices were rising strongly, many people decided not to sell their existing property but to let it. This takes your home out of the purely residential market and turns it into a commercial venture. Different rules then apply. As a landlord, you have to be professional in all your dealings with your tenants and you must comply with the law.

What a lettings agent does

If you decide to let your property, the first decision to make is whether to appoint a lettings agent to find a tenant or whether you will do it yourself. You will save a lot of money doing it yourself, because most agents charge a standard 10 per cent of the annual rental income plus VAT for introducing a tenant and an additional 5 per cent if they manage the property for you while it is let. Some charge even more. It is easier to let a flat than to sell one by yourself, but you need to understand how the market works. If you have not done this before, it would probably be better to appoint an agent. Agents offer different services in lettings and you need to pick the one that matches your needs.

Introducing tenants

This is the basic option. The agent will value the property for rental. They handle the marketing and find you a tenant. By the time they ring you with an offer, they should have an idea of the personal circumstances of the tenants, how long a tenancy they are looking for and some assessment of whether they are suitable tenants for the property.

The agent takes up the tenant's references on your behalf with employers and credit ratings agencies and prepares a tenancy agreement for both parties to sign. They also ensure that a deposit of either a month's or six weeks' rent is paid on the day the contract is signed and the keys to the property are handed over.

Deposits can be held either by the agent or the landlord for the duration of the tenancy and can be used to pay for the cost of any dilapidations that arise during the tenancy. This does not include normal wear and tear, but it does cover breakages that are the responsibility of the tenant and professional cleaning if the premises are not left in a pristine state.

Deposits are one of the most contentious issues between landlords and tenants, and there are frequent disagreements about what the landlord claims from it. Some tenants prefer that the agent hold their deposit because they have a better chance of getting it back, and some lettings agents insist on holding it. The risk to the landlord if the lettings agency goes out of business, means there will be no sum to fall back on for repairs.

The agent will organize that the necessary legal checks are carried out on the property. A CORGI-registered plumber has to check all the gas appliances once a year, and for safety an electrical check should also be carried out, although legal requirements are less stringent over electricity than with gas. The agent will also organize an inventory firm to carry out an inspection with the tenants when they move in to the property. You will have to settle all these fees yourself – they are not included in the commission payment.

Once the tenant moves in, you are responsible for managing the property. You have to check that the rent comes in on time and sort out any problems with maintenance.

Rent collection

Some agents will introduce a tenant and also collect the rent as part of the service. The standard charge for this is 12.5 per cent plus VAT. This puts a third party between the landlord and the tenant should there be any disputes over payments. The disadvantage is that the agent usually holds on to the rent for several days each month before releasing it into your account. This delay can be critical if you don't get the rent before the mortgage payment goes out, and it's not worth paying for this type of agent unless you sign up for the full management service.

Management service

Agents offer a management service for the duration of the tenancy in addition to introducing the tenant and collecting the rent, for which the standard charge is 15 per cent plus VAT. If there are any problems with the maintenance of the flat, they will send their contractors to sort it out. You will have to pay the bills for this, and it can work out more expensive than if you had organized it yourself. In theory, it is less work for the landlord, and you should consider this service if, say, you are going abroad or live some distance from the property. Managing agents can be slow to respond to tenants' request, and even from a distance you may find you end up doing much of the work yourself. Nobody is going to care about your property as much as you do.

Furnishing rental properties

Unfurnished flats have become much more popular in recent years. Young professionals in particular like to build up their own collection of furniture and want to escape from the memories of cheap, unattractive digs.

There is still plenty of demand for furnished accommodation, mostly from students or new graduates, who cannot afford to buy their own furniture, and from overseas visitors, who are staying for a relatively short period. People newly separated from their spouses or people between homes also often want furnished accommodation.

Fire regulations get tighter all the time, and all the furniture in a rental property must comply with modern standards, otherwise the landlord is liable for heavy fines. Be careful about buying at auction to furnish your properties. It is safer to approach furniture companies that specialize in supplying furniture to landlords. They cater for all budgets.

The disadvantage of providing furniture is that tenants never look after it well, and you should consider it as only having a short life. This is fine if you are furnishing a low-budget flat for which basic furniture from high-street stores is appropriate. It is more of a problem if you are offering accommodation to corporate tenants in a city's more expensive postcodes, where you have to match their aspirations in fitting out the flat. There is a risk that you spend so much on the furniture and appliances that you do not get an adequate return for your investment.

Even in unfurnished flats it is standard to include appliances, such as a refrigerator and a cooker, and also floor coverings, carpets and curtains. Storage, such as built-in wardrobes, is also often standard. Partially furnished flats offer beds and, sometimes, a sofa, coffee table and dining table and chairs. In all cases, the furniture and fittings should be in immaculate condition. If there is any doubt about the state of the carpets, you should replace them. Wooden floors and Venetian blinds withstand wear and tear better than carpets, and they are popular because they are neutral and fashionable. Tenants can add their own rugs if they want to.

Short-term lets

In major cities short-term lets are popular with visitors and corporate executives, who come for two or three months and don't want to stay in a hotel for such a long time. The rentals you can achieve with this type of letting are much higher than in a tenancy of more than six months – usually 50–100 per cent more – but this does not make short-term lets more profitable because the costs are much higher.

You have to furnish the flat throughout, and that includes providing cable or satellite TV as well as a fax and modem. The kitchen should be fully equipped, and you will have to provide bed linen. You also have to offer cleaning services at least once a week, and you have to pay all bills, including the telephone line, although you can make arrangements to cover the cost of the calls.

The commission to estate agents for this type of let is also much higher – it is typically 15–20 per cent depending on the length of the tenancy. The cost of your insurance premiums on the property and the contents will also rise to reflect the greater risk of claims. Wear and tear is also much higher, and furniture and fittings will have to be replaced much more quickly.

The biggest problem with short-term lets is that the void periods are likely to be much more frequent and longer than you get with a long-term tenancy. You will probably have no problem letting the property during the summer months and at holiday times, such as Christmas and Easter, but you may find that the flat is hard to let in autumn and winter, and this could erode all your profit from the higher rent.

You should probably consider short-term lets only if you have a flat in a central location, which is close to all amenities and popular with tourists and international visitors.

Troubleshooting

If you decide to manage the property yourself you will find that you don't have to do anything other than watch the rent come in for several months, but all too often small problems arise and will need attention, and you need to be able to respond quickly to your tenants' requests.

It is essential that you will be able to find some free time during the working day to meet plumbers or workmen at the site and stay with them while they work on the job. If your other commitments don't allow you to do this, you need to think about using an agent offering a management service. Problems arise most frequently with central heating or leaking baths and taps. You will need the phone numbers of several friendly plumbers who can be called out at short notice to fix the problems.

Difficult tenants

More serious issues arise when you have problems with rental payments. Most tenants are honest and responsible, but you will inevitably encounter the occasional bad tenant if you let property over a number of years. No matter how you choose to handle the situation, you must make sure that you are acting in compliance with landlord and tenant legislation. Consult a solicitor. Your regular solicitor may be able to give you some informal advice but should also be able to refer you to specialists if you need to take the tenant to court.

The best approach with non-paying tenants is to deal with them directly in the first instance and keep the relationship amicable. If their financial situation has changed, you need to persuade them to leave as soon as possible without doing any damage to your property. That is more likely to happen smoothly if you have a personal relationship with them and haven't fallen out with them.

Holiday lets

If you have a second home in a location that is popular with tourists, you may want to consider letting it to help offset the costs of maintenance. This can work well if you are highly organized, and you will need to use a specialist agent.

The first consideration is location. Some counties are particularly popular with holiday-makers in the UK, and you can rely on demand in the summer months always exceeding supply. These counties include Cornwall, Devon, Suffolk, Norfolk, Pembrokeshire and the Cotswolds. Some towns are also always in demand, especially where there is an influx of summer schools or visitors, such as Oxford, Stratford-upon-Avon and Brighton. Holiday lettings are usually for one week or two, and the turnover is high. It is your responsibility to make sure that the property is cleaned and the bedding changed for each new tenancy, and this means that you will need the services of a cleaner. Changeover day is usually Saturday and every other holiday cottage will need a cleaner on the same day, so the cost of the service is high.

A holiday lettings agency will find and vet tenants for you and manage the property to cover emergency repairs. They may introduce you to suitable cleaners in the area, but they will not take responsibility for the preparation of the property before the visitors arrive. They will, however, give you good advice on how to prepare your property for the holiday lets market, which can help you to get your house into a higher rental category. Their charges are high and usually about 20 per cent of the rental income.

Holiday lets are always furnished and must comply with fire regulations. You also have to provide furniture that you may not need but some of your tenants will, such as a cot for a young child and twin beds in at least one bedroom. You should also include satellite TV and some games for children. The wear and tear on the property and furnishings will be high and will erode your profit substantially. There is a high level of breakages, inevitably, and you should put in sturdy washing machines and dishwashers that can stand a fair amount of abuse from visitors unfamiliar with the machines' individual quirks.

The other disadvantage of holiday letting is that it restricts when you can use the property. If a holiday letting agency agrees to take it on their books, they will want to have access to it for the whole of the season, which can run from March (or at least Easter) through to October and may also include Christmas and New Year. You will be allowed to specify a certain number of weeks for your own use (usually six to eight weeks in a year), but you have to notify them of your chosen weeks months in advance. All flexibility and spontaneity is lost.

The advantage of letting your holiday home through an agency is that it does stop friends or friends of friends from asking to use it for free and running up large electricity and heating bills with little or no recompense. The disadvantages are that you may also dislike the fact that the property ceases to feel like your home and you have to leave it ready for visitors rather than you just walking into it the next weekend.

To comply with Inland Revenue conditions for tax relief on the costs of running the property, the house has to be available for letting for 140 days a year at a commercial rate and be let for at least 70 days. The same tenant can be *in situ* for only 31 days.

Bed and breakfast

This is a useful way of earning extra cash. People making short trips away from home often prefer to stay in a B&B rather than a hotel because they are usually cheaper and friendlier places. It does require good organization on your part if it is not to become too onerous, and you must be prepared to sacrifice some privacy.

You must have a suitable house of a certain size. People prefer *en-suite* bathrooms, but if you cannot manage that, the guest bathroom should be separate from your own.

If you are letting out up to two rooms, the market is unregulated. When you let more than that number you have to comply with fire regulations. The English Tourist Board provides information packs on how to get started. If you want to register your property with them, they will carry out an inspection and grade the property according to the standard of the amenities you can offer your customers.

The Inland Revenue will regard this as a commercial business, and you can offset many of the setting-up and running costs against your taxable income. Take advice from an experienced accountant because it is complicated.

Lodgers

If you let a room to a lodger you do not have to pay tax on the first £4,250 of rental income. There will be no formal tenancy agreement with a lodger because you are resident in the house. State your terms and conditions clearly when you are reaching an agreement and state the price for the room. The key issues will be access to the remainder of the house. You need to decide how much you want the lodger to be part of the family and set the rules accordingly.

Summary: Letting a Property

Using a lettings agent

The three levels of service and usual cost plus VAT are:

- **Introducing tenants:** 10 per cent.
- **Rent collection:** 12.5 per cent.
- **Management service:** 15 per cent.

Furnishing rental properties

Floor coverings, curtains and appliances are standard in all properties and must comply with fire regulations.

Short-term lets

- Rentals are much higher but so are costs: agent fees, insurance, furnishings and equipment (which must be comprehensive).
- Voids are likely to be long and more frequent.
- Only consider if your property is very central and suitable for corporate tenants.

Managing problems yourself

If you have bad tenants, consult a solicitor to ensure you comply with the law. Deal with them directly – try to keep relations amicable.

Holiday lets

Location determines suitability. Wear and tear on the property is high and your access may be restricted. You need to use a specialist agent.

Bed and breakfast

The English Tourist board supplies starter packs and carries out inspections. The Inland Revenue regards it as a commercial business.

Lodgers

The first £4,250 of rent is tax free. There is no formal tenancy agreement, so state your terms and conditions clearly.

Part 5

Useful Addresses and Websites

Useful Addresses and Websites

Architects

Royal Institute of British
Architects
66 Portland Place
London
W1B 4AD
Tel: 020 7580 5533
www.architecture.com

Association of Consultant
Architects
98 Hayes Road
Bromley
Kent
BR2 9AB
Tel: 020 8325 1402

Royal Institution of
Chartered Surveyors
RICS Contact Centre
Surveyor Court
Westwood Way
Coventry
CV4 8JE
Tel: 0870 333 1600
www.rics.org.uk

Edinburgh Architectural
Association
15 Rutland Square
Edinburgh
EH1 2BE
Tel: 0131 229 7545
www.edarch.demon.co.uk
/direct.html

Building materials and information

The Building Centre
26 Store Street
London
WC1E 7BT
Tel: 020 7692 6209
www.buildingcentre.co.uk

National Home Improvement
Advisory Service
1 Bondgate
Helmsley
Yorkshire
YO26 6RW
01439 771462
www.nrwas.com

Federation of Master Builders
Gordon Fisher House
14–15 Great James Street
London
WC1N 3DP
Tel: 020 7242 7583
www.fmb.org.uk

National Inspection Council
for Electrical Installation
Contracting
37 Albert Embankment
London
SE1 7UJ
Tel: 020 7564 2323
www.niceic.org.uk

Electrical Contractors
Association Ltd
Esca House
34 Palace Court
London
W2 4HY
Tel: 020 7313 4800
www.eca.co.uk

National Federation of
Roofing Contractors
24 Weymouth Street
London
W1G 7LX
Tel: 020 7436 0387
www.nfrc.co.uk

Flat Roofing Alliance
Fields House
Gower Road
Haywards Heath
West Sussex
RH16 4PL
Tel: 01444 440027
www.fra.org.uk

Institute of Plumbing
64 Station Lane
Hornchurch
Essex
RM12 6NB
Tel: 01708 472791
www.plumbers.org.uk

Institute of Domestic
Heating and Environmental
Engineers (IDHE)
Dorchester House
Wimblestraw Road
Brimfield
Wallingford
Oxon
OX10 7LZ
Tel: 01865 343096
www.idhe.org.uk

Central Heating
Information Council
36 Holly Walk
Leamington Spa
Warwickshire
CV32 4LY
Tel: 0845 600 2200
www.centralheating.co.uk

Association of Plumbing and
Heating Contractors (APHC)
14 Ensign House
Ensign Business Centre
Westwood Way
Coventry
CV4 8JA
Tel: 0800 542 6060
www.aphc.co.uk

Heating and Ventilating
Contractors' Association
(HVCA)
Esca House
34 Palace Court
London W2 4JG
Tel: 020 7313 4900
Fax: 020 7727 9268
www.hvca.org.uk

British Gas
30 The Causeway
Staines
Middlesex
TW18 3BY
Tel: 0845 775 4754
www.gas.co.uk
www.house.co.uk

Council for Registered Gas
Installers (CORGI)
1 Elmwood
Chineham Business Park
Crockford Lane
Basingstoke
Hampshire
RG24 8WG
Tel: 0870 401 2200
www.corgi-gas.com

Ecomerchant Ltd
The Old Filling Station
Head Hill Road
Goodnestone
near Faversham
Kent
ME13 9BY
Tel: 01795 530130
www.ecomerchant.co.uk

Screwfix
www.screwfix.com

Wickes Building Supplies Ltd
Tel: 0500 300 328
www.wickes.co.uk

Windows and skylights

Anglian Windows
Tel: 0800 500 600
ww.anglianwindows.co.uk

British Woodworking Federation
56–64 Leonard Street
London
EC2A 4JX
Tel: 020 7608 5050
www.bwf.org.uk

Everest Ltd
www.everest.co.uk

Glass and Glazing Federation
44–48 Borough High Street
London
SE1 1XB
Tel: 020 7403 7177
www.ggf.org.uk

National Replacement Windows
Advisory Service
Tel: 0800 028 5809
www.nrwas.com

The Original Boxsash
Window Co.
Tel: 0800 783 4053
www.boxsash.com

Velux Company Ltd
Woodside Way
Glenrothes East
Fife, KY7 4ND
Tel: 01592 772211
www.velux.com

Self-build

Buildstore
www.buildstore.co.uk
Useful website for self-builders,
offering plotsearch, mortgage
finance and building supplies

Nordic timber
www.woodforgood.com
Campaign to promote the use of
Nordic timber in construction

Self-build web directory
www.ebuild.co.uk
UK self-build, DIY and house
renovations

Home building and renovating
www.homebuilding.co.uk
Includes: case studies, beginners
guide and directory of suppliers

Specialist construction

Back to Front Exterior Design
37 West Street
Farnham
Surrey
GU9 7DR
Tel: 01252 820984
www.backtofrontexteriordesign.
com

London Basement Company Ltd
Innovation House
292 Worton Road
Isleworth
Middlesex
TW7 6EL
Tel: 020 8847 9449
www.tlbc.co.uk

Basement Force
River Reach
1 Gartons Way
London
SW11 3SX
Tel: 020 7924 1434
www.forcefoundations.co.uk
www.basementforce.co.uk

Conservatories

**National Conservatory
Advisory Service**
Tel: 0800 028 5809
www.nrwas.com

Swimming pools

**Swimming Pool and Allied
Trades Association**
1a Junction Road
Andover
Hampshire
SP10 3QT
Tel: 01264 356210
www.spata.co.uk

Plastica
www.plastica.ltd.uk
A trade supplier only of all
swimming pool equipment; the
website has a useful dealer
network list to find suppliers in
your area

House and garden

Home and garden products
www.homeandgardening.co.uk
Useful website providing a
comprehensive shopping
directory for home and gardens

Garden Advice
www.gardenadvice.co.uk
Advice for members by e-mail

National chains

B&Q
Tel: 0845 222 1000
www.diy.com

Homebase
Tel: 0870 900 8098
www.homebase.co.uk

Ikea
www.ikea.co.uk

Magnet
www.magnet.co.uk

MFI
www.mfi.co.uk

Kitchen suppliers

Kitchen Specialists Association
Tel: 01905 726066
www.kbsa.co.uk
Help with finding kitchen
designers and suppliers

Alternative Plans Ltd
9 Hester Road
London
SW11 4AN
Tel: 020 7228 6460

Four Seasons Design
149a Street Lane
Roundhay
Leeds
LS8 1AA
Tel: 0113 294 1414

Fulham Kitchens & Furniture
19 Carnwarth Road
London
SW6 3HR
Tel: 020 7736 6458

Heal's
196 Tottenham Court Road
London
W1T 7LQ
Tel: 020 7636 1666
www.heals.co.uk

John Lewis
Oxford Street
London
W1A 1EX
Tel: 020 7629 7711
www.johnlewis.com

The Kitchen Consultancy
Stadium House
21–23 Bath Road
London
N9 0JX
Tel: 07974 149997

Plain English Design Ltd
41a Hoxton Square
London
N1 6PB
Tel: 020 7613 0022

The Shaker Workshop
The Workshop
Barcham Farm
Soham
Ely
Cambridgeshire
CB7 5TU
Tel: 01353 624616
www.theshakerworkshop.co.uk

Smallbone of Devizes
Hopton Industrial Estate
London Road
Devizes
Wiltshire
SN10 2EU
Tel: 01380 729090
www.smallbone.co.uk

Space Savers
222 Kentish Town Road
London
NW5 2AD
Tel: 020 7485 3266
www.spacesaver.co.uk

Mark Wilkinson
Overton House
High Street
Bromham
near Chippenham
Wiltshire
SN15 2HA
Tel: 01380 850004
www.mwf.com

Bathrooms

Antique Baths
Erme Bridge Works
Ermington Road
Ivybridge
Devon
PL21 9DE
Tel: 01752 698250
www.antiquebaths.com

Armitage Shanks
Tel: 01543 490253
www.armitage-shanks.co.uk

Aston Matthews
141–147a Essex Road
London
N1 2SN
Tel: 020 7226 7220
www.astonmatthews.co.uk

Chris Stevens Ltd
545–561 Holloway Road
London
N19 4BT
Tel: 020 7272 1228

C.P. Hart
Newnham Terrace
Hercules Road
London
SE1 7DR
Tel: 020 7902 1000
www.cphart.co.uk

Creative Bathrooms
Pendals Close
Hampstead Norreys
Berkshire
RG18 0TR
Tel: 01635 200068
www.creativebathrooms.co.uk

Dolphin Bathrooms
Tel: 0800 626 717
www.dolphinbathrooms.com

Ideal Standard Ltd
The Bathroom Works
National Avenue
Hull
HU5 4HS
Tel: 01482 346461
www.ideal-standard.co.uk

Twyford Bathrooms
Lawton Road
Alsager
Stoke-on-Trent
Staffordshire
ST7 2DF
Tel: 01270 873 864
www.twyfordbathrooms.com

Lighting

Lighting Association
Stafford Park 7
Telford
Shropshire
TF3 3BQ
Tel: 01952 290905
www.lightingassociation.com

DPA Lighting Consultants
24 City Business Centre
Lower Road
London
SE16 2XB
Tel: 020 7252 3372
www.dpalighting.com

John Cullen Lighting
585 King's Road
London
SW6 2EH
Tel: 020 7371 5400
www.johncullenlighting.co.uk

The London Lighting Company
135 Fulham Road
London
SW3 6RT
Tel: 020 7589 3612

Paint

Crown Paints
Tel: 0870 240 1127
www.crownpaint.co.uk

Dulux
ICI Paints Plc
Wexham Road
Slough
Berkshire
SL2 5DS
Tel: 01753 550555
www.dulux.co.uk

Farrow and Ball
Uddens Estate
Wimborne
Dorset
BH21 7NL
Tel: 01202 876141
www.farrow-ball.com

International Paints
Tel: 01480 484 284
www.international-paints.co.uk
Specialist paints for fridges,
radiators, melamine and tiles

John Oliver
33 Pembridge Road
London
W11 3HG
Tel: 020 7221 6466
www.johnoliver.co.uk

Paint and Paper Library
5 Elystan Street
London
SW3 3NT
Tel: 020 7823 7755
www.paintlibrary.co.uk

Tile and stone

Fired Earth Tiles Plc
Twyford Mill
Oxford Road
Adderbury
Oxon
OX17 3HP
Tel: 01295 814315
www.firedearth.co.uk

H. & R. Johnson Tiles
Harewood Street
Tunstall
Stoke-on-Trent
Staffordshire
ST6 5JZ
Tel: 01782 575575
www.johnson-tiles.com

Porcelanosa
The Carr Carriage Drive
Doncaster
DN4 5NT
Tel: 0800 915 4000
www.porcelanosa.co.uk

Original Stone Company
100–105 Victoria Crescent
Burton-upon-Trent
Staffordshire
DE14 2QF
Tel: 01283 501090
www.originalstoneco.co.uk

Stonell
www.stonell.com

Tower Ceramics
91 Parkway
London
NW1 7PP
Tel: 020 7485 7192

World's End Tiles
Silverthorne Road
London
SW8 3HE
Tel: 020 7819 2110
www.worldsendtiles.co.uk

Carpets and flooring

Altro Floors
Works Road
Letchworth
Hertfordshire
SG6 1NW
Tel: 01462 480480
www.altro.co.uk

Carpetright
www.carpetright.co.uk

Amtico Company
Solar Park
Southside
West Midlands
B90 4SH
Tel: 0121 745 0800
www.amtico.com

The Hardwood Flooring
Company
146–152 West End Lane
London
NW6 1SD
Tel: 020 7328 8481
www.hardwoodflooringcompany.
com

Junckers Ltd
Unit A
1 Wheaton Road
Witham
Essex
CM8 3UJ
Tel: 01376 534700
www.junckers.co.uk

Kahrs UK
Unit 2 West
68 Bognor Road
Chichester
West Sussex
PO19 8NS
Tel: 01243 778747
www.kahrs.com

Solid Floor
53 Pembridge Road
London
W11 3GH
Tel: 020 7221 9166
www.solidfloor.co.uk

Fabrics and furnishings

Crowson Fabrics
Crowson House
Bellbrook Park
Uckfield
East Sussex
TN22 1QZ
Tel: 01825 761044
www.crowsonfabrics.com

Dorma
PO Box 7
Lees Street
Swinton
Manchester
M27 6DB
Tel: 0161 251 4468
www.dorma.co.uk
Bedroom fabrics and
accessories

G P & J Baker
G P & J Baker House
6 Stinsford Road
Poole
Dorset
BH17 0SW
Tel: 01202 266700
www.gpjbaker.co.uk
Top-quality curtain and
upholstery fabrics

Harlequin Fabrics and
Wallcoverings
Ladybird House
Beeches Road
Loughborough
Leicestershire
LE11 2HA
Tel: 08708 300355
www.harlequin.uk.com

Sanderson
Sanderson House
Oxford Road
Buckinghamshire
UB9 4DX
Tel: 01895 830000
Fabrics and wallcoverings

House doctors

The Final Touch London Ltd
12 St John's Hill Grove
London
SW11 2RG
Tel: 020 7228 4233
www.thefinaltouch.co.uk

Home Stagers
Tel: 01295 770588
www.homestagers.co.uk

Property Presentation
Tel: 0800 542 8952
www.propertypresentation.co.uk

Property search websites

www.assertahome.com
www.fish4homes.com
www.primelocation.com
www.propertyfinder.co.uk
www.upmystreet.com
www.loot.com
www.thisislondon.co.uk
www.ukpropertyshop.co.uk
www.your-move.co.uk

Property sale websites

www.eBay.co.uk
www.armchairproperty.com
www.propertybrokers.com
www.property-sale-
directory.co.uk
www.propertysalewales.co.uk
www.smartnewhomes.com

Estate agents

FPD Savills
www.fpdsavills.co.uk

Hamptons International
www.hamptons.co.uk

Foxtons
www.foxtons.com

Knight Frank
www.knightfrank.co.uk

National Association of Estate
Agents
www.naea.co.uk

Ombudsman for Estate Agents
Scheme
www.oea.co.uk

Strutt and Parker
www.struttandparker.co.uk

Association of Residential
Letting Agents
Maple House
53–55 Woodside Road
Amersham
Buckinghamshire
HP6 6AA
Tel: 0845 345 5752
www.arla.co.uk

Location agents

The Location Company
1 Charlotte Street
London
W1P 1HD
Tel: 020 7637 7766
www.thelocation.co.uk

Planning advice and information

Planning information
www.planning.odpm.gov.uk

Inland Revenue
www.inlandrevenue.gov.uk

Commonhold and Leasehold
Reform
www.commonhold.com

Energy Saving Trust
Tel: 0800 512 012
www.est.org.uk

Clear Skies
Tel: 0870 243 0930
www.clear-skies.org

Information on old and listed properties

Asbestos Removal
Davis Environmental Ltd
Head Office
Church Farm
Hospital Lane
Warwickshire
CV12 OJ2
Tel: 07976 684717

The Department of Culture,
Media and Sport
(listed Buildings)
www.culture.gov.uk/heritage/ind
ex.html

English Heritage
Customer Services Department
PO Box 569
Swindon
SN2 2YP
Tel: 0870 333 1181

Save Britain's Heritage
70 Cowcross Street
London
EC1M 6EJ
Tel: 020 7253 3500
www.savebritainsheritage.org/
main.htm

Georgian Group
6 Fitzroy Square
London
W1T 5DX
Tel: 020 7529 8920
www.georgiangroup.org.uk

Victorian Society
1 Priory Gardens
Bedford Park
London
W4 1TT
Tel: 020 8994 1019
www.victoriansociety.org.uk

Twentieth Century Society
70 Cowcross Street
London
EC1M 6EJ
Tel: 020 7250 3857
www.c20society.demon.co.uk

Society for the Protection of
Ancient Buildings
37 Spital Square
London
E1 6DY
Tel: 020 7377 1644
www.spab.org.uk

Watchdogs

The Good Housekeeping
Institute
Tel: 0906 752 9070
www.goodhousekeeping.co.uk
/ghi.html

Bibliography

Sunday Times: Small Spaces for Modern Living
Caroline Atkins, Hamlyn, 2003

Building Your Own Home
Murray Armor and David Snell (Editor),
Ebury Press, 2002

Property Ladder
Sarah Beeny, Cassell, 2002

Guide to Renovating Your Home
Alison Cork, Piatkus 1995

Planning: A Guide for Householders
Allison Flight, Planning Aid for London, 1995

Fiona Fullerton's Guide to Buying, Selling and
Moving House
Fiona Fullerton, Piatkus Books, 2003

Great Renovations: A New Life for Older Homes
Mary Gilliatt, Watson-Guptill Publications, 2003

Home Extensions: The Complete Handbook
Paul Hymers, New Holland Publishers, 2002

Old House Rescue Book: Buying and Renovating
on a Budget
Robert Kangas, Reston Pub Co, 1982

Selling Houses: How to Sell Your House as Quickly
as You Can for as Much Money as You Can
Anthea Masey and Andrew Winter, Headline, 2004

Deck Planner: 120 Outstanding Decks
You Can Build
Scott Millard, Home Planners Inc, 2002

Renovating Old Houses
George Nash, The Taunton Press, 2004

The Penguin Dictionary of Building
James Maclean and John Scott (eds), 1993

Garden Design Bible
Tim Newbury, Hamlyn, 2004

Buying and Running a Small Hotel: The Complete
Guide to Setting Up and Managing Your Own
Hotel, Guest House or B & B
Ken Parker, How To Books, 2000

The Readers Digest Complete Do-It-Yourself
Manual
Readers Digest Association, 1996

The Readers Digest Illustrated Guide to Gardens
Readers Digest Association, 2000

The Readers Digest Repair Manual
Readers Digest Association, 1996

On Time and On Budget: A Home Renovation
Survival Guide
John Rusk, Main Street Books, 1997

Build Like a Pro: Expert Advice from Start to
Finish: Building a Deck
Scott Schuttner, The Taunton Press, 2002

The New London Property Guide
Carrie Segrave, Mitchell Beazley (published annually)

The Handyman's Practical Guide to Renovating
Houses for Increasing Value and Profit
Gerald E. Sherwood, Research and Education
Association, 2002

Building Regulations in Brief
Ray Tricker, Butterworth Heinemann, 2004

Buying a House: A Step-by-Step Guide to
Buying Your Ideal Home
Adam Walker, How To Books, 1999

Home Extension: Planning, Managing and
Completing Your Extension
Laurie Williamson, The Croswood Press, 2000

Index

Acknowledgements

I am deeply grateful to the following for their advice and encouragement: Karen Robinson, Rhiannon Eland, Steve Fallon, Clare Hogg, Christina Probert-Jones, Michael Rothschild, Sebastian Scotney, Richard Vines, Andrea Whittaker, Joanna Wilsher and Barbara Schmitz, and to Doreen Palamartschuk-Gillon and Sarah Ford at Hamlyn.

Executive Editors Doreen Palamartschuk-Gillon and Sarah Ford
Project Editor Jessica Cowie
Executive Art Editor Karen Sawyer
Designer Peter Gerrish
Illustrators Stephen Dew, Jason Cook
Production Controller Ian Paton